VERTICAL TAKE-OFF

This book is dedicated to the men and women of British Aerospace who saw change as an opportunity, not a threat

VERTICAL
TAKE-OFF

The inside story of
British Aerospace's comeback
from crisis to world class

SIR RICHARD EVANS

and

COLIN PRICE

NICHOLAS BREALEY
PUBLISHING

LONDON

First published by
Nicholas Brealey Publishing Limited in 1999

36 John Street   1163 E. Ogden Avenue, Suite 705-229
London   Naperville
WC1N 2AT, UK   IL 60563-8535, USA
Tel: +44 (0)171 430 0224   Tel: (888) BREALEY
Fax: +44 (0)171 404 8311   Fax: (630) 428 3442
http://www.nbrealey-books.com

© PricewaterhouseCoopers 1999
The right of PricewaterhouseCoopers to be identified as the
author of this work has been asserted in accordance with the
Copyright, Designs and Patents Act 1988.

ISBN 1-85788-245-8

British Library Cataloguing in Publication Data
A catalogue record for this book is available from the
British Library.

Printed in Finland by WSOY.

CONTENTS

Foreword
Lord Blyth of Rowington, Chairman – The Boots Company plc   vii
Preface   ix

1   The Poisoned Chalice   1
2   Who We Are and What We Stand For   24
3   When Change Management Works –
     and When It Doesn't   44
4   The Value Teams Go to Work   62
5   High-Integrity Implementation   86
6   Now for the Nuts and Bolts – the Benchmark Actions   106
7   Paradoxes, Enablers and Role Models of
     Culture Change   133
8   The Power Train Delivers   148
9   What Gets Measured Gets Done   182
10   The Pay-Off   195

Epilogue: The Future of Benchmark
John Weston, Chief Executive   205
Index   211

"The success of British Aerospace is one of the great unsung stories of our times. Seven years ago it was on the ropes. The country's biggest employer and exporter, and one of its supreme technological organisations, was on the edge of a crash.

A new management team headed by Dick Evans made a spectacular comeback, turned BAe into one of the most efficient aerospace companies in the world. One of the springboards of this achievement has been the sweeping culture change programme, called Benchmark BAe, which is the subject of this book.

In this story we see the same qualities that make Dick and his team such exemplary managers: thoroughness, self-criticism, creativity and cunning. Managing a change of culture is one of the most demanding, but essential Management Skills."

Sir John Harvey Jones

FOREWORD

Lord Blyth of Rowington
Chairman – The Boots Company plc

Anyone who is or ever might be involved in a culture change effort should read *Vertical Take-Off*. I promise that it will save them a lot of grief. One message that radiates from its pages is the intractability of the culture change problem. No one who reads this book will ever, in his or her life, underestimate the size of the mountain. Big-scale change in large organisations is definitely not for the faint-hearted, or those looking for quick fixes, or lacking deep pockets. But this narrative demonstrates that provided it is conceived and executed with managerial rigour, culture change – significant and durable – can add massively to the bottom line and to value for shareholders.

I have known Dick Evans for twenty years. Originally he was my customer when I was running Lucas Aerospace. Then he was my co-negotiator on the Al Yamamah project – I was head of Defence Sales at the Ministry of Defence and Dick was the Managing Director of British Aerospace at Warton. Thirdly, he was a board colleague at BAe from 1990–94 and today we are again board colleagues at NatWest Group.

A journalist once described Dick as 'the sort of affable host you might find behind the bar of a friendly northern golf club'. The appearance is deceptive. Genial and unflappable though he is, Dick Evans is hugely smart, a great negotiator and he genuinely has strategic vision about the aerospace business. 1990–94 were dark years indeed for BAe, years in which the company barely survived. Dick Evans was a relatively inexperienced chief executive, untested by the burdens of running a large-scale complex organisation with diverse constituencies. But throughout the crises, he never lost his customary aplomb nor his conviction that the company would pull through. He staunched the haemorrhaging and established the the fact that he was much more than a super salesman of defence equipment. What could hardly be imagined when I left the BAe board, with Dick firmly in charge, was the magnitude of the turn-around that he would achieve in the years that followed. That turnaround was accompanied by a tripling of the share price. And one of the forces behind his success is the subject of this book: a sweeping culture change programme that has forged strong corporate unity where it was sorely lacking, overwhelming the divisional 'baronies' and creating a cohesive and smoothly functioning machine.

Most accounts of change management are big on slogans and short on details. They proclaim the change message with a sound of trumpets, quickly rattle off some bromides about 'empowerment', hand out posters and T-shirts and declare victory. It is typical of Dick to tell the story of this ambitious project warts and all. He spotlights the obstacles and problems met along the way and shows how remedies were painstakingly delivered. The result is a credible and fascinating document, probably unique in British industry. Ably supported by co-author Colin Price, Dick Evans offers a blow-by-blow account of a long, five-year march that is still not over, since he candidly admits to its shortcomings and unfinished agenda.

PREFACE

Bitish Aerospace has been much in the news because of speculation about the future course of European and global aerospace and defence consolidation, and our £7.8 billion merger with Marconi Electronics. This book is not about either topic directly. Its subject is a force, unmentioned in the newspaper headlines, that stands behind much of our recent success.

The name of this force is BenchmarkBAe, a five-year culture-change project that has powered a turnaround of some magnitude. Without this sweeping effort at culture change, the stark fact is that BAe would not today be part of the discussions on defence industry restructuring and rationalisation. The debate would be going on without us, because we would have remained (had we even survived as an independent company) a weak and marginal player. When I sit in on these meetings, I'm conscious of how deeply Benchmark is a key factor in the strength of our negotiating positions. No matter how the industry's consolidations play out in future – who merges with whom, what consortia and joint ventures are created – Benchmark will have helped determine favourable outcomes for our employees and shareholders.

While the value of culture change programmes is not on the radar of most security analysts, Benchmark's economic results have been observed by many of our European competitors. If imitation is the sincerest form of flattery, then we should be flattered that some rivals on the Continent that seven years ago had written off BAe in the context of the future of this industry are now seriously doing, or contemplating, similar programmes. Personnel in at least three of our joint ventures have had some exposure to culture change – Airbus Industrie, the Eurofighter partnership and Matra BAe Dynamics. In the past many of our senior managers seconded to these partnerships returned to the BAe parent to participate in the change experience. And on going back to work, they helped in the transmission of our values and also in seeding programmes that were similar in intent.

Benchmark also has a major role to play in the BAe/Marconi combination. It is one of the chief enablers that will deliver the synergies and expected benefits of this merger. We will create a lot more shareholder value than would be possible without it. I say this with great confidence because the fates have been kind. Programmes very like Benchmark are already growing in the soil of Marconi Electronics and its parent GEC – though they are less evolved than Benchmark, by a few years. One of our key executives who helped give birth to Benchmark left to go over to them and our consultant and the co-author of *Vertical Take-Off*, Colin Price, has advised the company. So when we talk to the Marconi guys on the details of the impending integration, we start with the advantage of knowing their dedication to pushing culture change and of their familiarity with Benchmark's values and means of expression.

If I were to distil all the results of our culture change push into a single word, it would be pride. In the early 1990s this company lost its self-respect and its pride. We had been given a legacy by predecessors who had played key roles in the history of powered flight – the buccaneering types who had founded and nurtured great names like Hawker, Blackburn, Sopwith and those who followed after. And we very nearly blew that legacy when the company skirted the precipice of bankruptcy. Thanks to Benchmark, our pride is now restored and we have a rich and enduring inheritance to pass on to the younger people in our company.

Sir Richard Evans
Farnborough
April 1999

1
THE POISONED CHALICE

The New Year party of 1990 was a particularly happy one for me. That day I became Chief Executive of British Aerospace (BAe), the culmination of a lifetime career in the aerospace industry, mostly spent in marketing positions. British Aerospace was a very young company, cobbled together by the nationalisation of half a dozen defence and aerospace firms in 1977. Two years later, it was the first government-owned company launched by Prime Minister Thatcher's privatisation initiative.

At the beginning of 1990, as far I could see, the shortcomings and problems that existed in the company were not of much greater severity than those faced by the typical incoming chief executive to a large enterprise. The company had not done badly throughout most of the 1980s. The order book was healthy. The shares were middling performers in the FT-SE 100. Personally and corporately, there seemed to be a lot to celebrate that New Year.

At the end of my first year on the job, company sales and profits had increased and I was able to tell shareholders that 'the company's resilience against the background of uncertainty and change in the environment had been amply demonstrated'. I was confident that we would continue to thrive in the future.

Trouble on all sides

Just one year later, my mood and BAe's share price had plummeted. Trouble came from all sides: our property company was hit with a lousy market. Sales of the Rover Group sank by about a fifth and losses mounted. The government's defence spending volumes underwent a major review. Losses in our commercial aerospace division increased dramatically with the recession in the airline industry.

To keep the doors open, we needed capital, badly. In the autumn of 1991, we went to the City and raised £430 million from a rights issue. This was poorly received by investors and sent the stock into a long-term decline. The company's survival hung by a thread. As the problems mounted, major management changes were made. The chairman and finance director departed. I survived, barely.

Things got worse. In mid-1992 British Aerospace recorded the then biggest single asset write-off in UK corporate history – £1 billion, most of it for a restructuring of Regional Aircraft.

It was clear to me that I'd been given a poisoned chalice to drink from. As the share price fell to an all-time low of £0.97, down significantly from the rights issue price of £3.80, dividends were slashed to the bone. Shareholders who had stuck with us, believing our assurances of previous years that BAe was a worthwhile investment, were understandably upset. A hostile takeover from General Electric Co. seemed a very real possibility, because the shares were so cheap.

We immediately had to eliminate huge amounts of costs from the business, which could only be done by closing and reducing the size of many of our facilities and shedding thousands from the workforce. Understandably, there was a lot of political and media flack, much of it directed at me personally. One Member of Parliament was quoted in the press thus: 'I think management should all resign as a block for taking the shareholders' money and pissing it against the wall.'

'Dick Evans, the chief executive of British Aerospace, is coming under pressure to resign or to move to a lesser role within the group' was the lead on one newspaper story, which went on to quote a major BAe shareholder: 'He is not the flavour of the month. He is really a salesman, not a chief executive.'

The week following the £1 billion write-off, I visited Scotland to explain our situation to some leading Scottish institutions, long-term shareholders who had seen the value of large BAe holdings take one hell of a beating. During the nearly three years of my stewardship, the price had dropped by almost two-thirds. I had to face the music and give an assessment of the situation to the invest-ment community. Our first stop was Edinburgh, where our recep-tion was a chilly as the prevailing winds down Princes Street. In Glasgow that afternoon, facing a group of analysts and institu-tional investors, I was barely a minute into my presentation when the red-faced senior investment manager across the table from me stood up, shook his fists in the air and railed at me. Pandemonium ensued. The meeting came to a halt and embarrassment hung heavy in the air. The out-of-control investment manager was frog-marched from the room and I was asked – perhaps out of pity – to continue the presentation. This was not an isolated incident. On other occasions I was treated with less than the customary proto-col for the chief of a major firm. At another meeting with institu-tional holders, I was shocked when I entered the room and the head man said frostily, 'We're all very busy people, so let's skip the handshakes, and get down to business.' After we left, going down in the lift, I turned to my investment relations chief and said, 'If you have any more bright ideas like this one, please keep them to yourself.'

I and others in the top management team seemed to be on the ropes almost every day, continually fire-fighting, speeding from crisis to crisis. As if the shame of the write-off were not enough, we had to endure the wrenching pain of further asset dispositions and job redundancies and the consequent economic devastation of several communities. Recessionary forces hit every single one of our business sectors simultaneously and the end of the Cold War spelled the long-term atrophy of the defence business. Through restructuring we eliminated 60,000 out of 127,000 jobs that were on the payroll when I took over, more than 40,000 of them in regional aircraft alone. We leant over backwards and went as far as we could in financial terms to make the separation palatable to those who had to be let go, so they could leave with a certain amount of dignity. That we had some success in this regard is reflected in the fact that we had no industrial relations problems at all during this period.

Yet it was not difficult for me to imagine what people were saying about BAe in the pubs and on the unemployment lines of towns where we'd long been a source of strength. And basically I agreed with them. They'd had a rotten deal. So had the investors, and so had I. Although chief executive of the nation's best-known technology and defence company, I was a pariah in the City and on the high streets of towns where British Aerospace had once been the economic lifeblood. Nothing in my previous experience in business could have prepared me for the exigencies, pains and humiliations of this period. During the worst of it, the board would have had cause to fire me. They chose not to do so, largely, I suspect, because there was no candidate in his right mind who'd have stepped into my shoes.

There was no shortage of grit and guts in the BAe management team. The sleepless nights, the crisis management marathons, the feeling of every day waking up with a large boulder on one's chest, would all be justified one day – we were sure of that. We'd get even with fate. True, we also had feelings of inadequacy: natural enough, given our lack of control over events. But as we tackled and tamed each problem, it was not the inadequacy that was uppermost, it was self-confidence and *esprit de corps*. By the orderliness of our retreats we proved to ourselves (if to no one else) that we were pretty good fighters and good managers. Although this was the most difficult period of my career, and one I would not want to live through again, I never doubted that we'd solve the underlying problems. And from this there would emerge, like a phoenix, a revivified national asset.

Someone once said that 'living well is the best revenge'. Our revenge would be to effect a comeback and then go one step further and transform British Aerospace into a leading player in every one of the factors that determine competitive success. Realistically, this was at that time an almost absurd ambition. In many dimensions of business we were far from excellent practitioners. Fortunately in many key areas, such as productivity and innovation, our rivals in aerospace weren't such hot shots either.

Strengths and weaknesses

The aura of a great past permeated BAe. Here under one corporate roof one found many of the great names of aviation history, going back to the dawn of powered flight, including the British Aircraft Corporation (my alma mater), De Havilland, Bristol, Sopwith, Glosters, English Electric, Cambra and Lightning, Vickers, Hawker, Scottish Aviation, Avro. These forerunners of modern aeronautics could point to great achievements in aviation such as the Viscount, in 1948 the first turbine-powered commercial airliner which, at its peak, was operated by three score airlines around the world; the Comet, the world's first commercial jet; the Harrier jet fighter, a world-class technological accomplishment in vertical/short take-off and landing, which entered service with the RAF in 1969. Upgraded Harrier variants fly today with the British Air Force and Royal Navy and the US Marine Corps.

Then there is that beautiful bird the Concorde, the first and only successful supersonic airliner, which flies daily between Britain and the US. Other famous contemporary aircraft from the BAe stable are the Hawk and the Tornado, part of a product line that is the most comprehensive of any manufacturer in the world. Overall, BAe's capabilities were a great resource for the nation, militarily and economically, as the country's biggest exporter of manufactured products and largest employer.

To offset the effects of dependence on erratic defence spending and improve the balance sheet, previous top management acquired an assortment of commercial firms, several at bargain prices. Their rationale was that these companies would be counter-cyclical to periodic weak revenues in the defence sector. Best known of these operations was the Rover Group, which was in the throes of an impressive comeback in product quality and customer service when I took over. Other acquisitions included Royal Ordnance, a solid performer with a monopoly on munitions supply to the British government, and Arlington Securities, a fast-growing property development company. The other strings to the BAe bow included a promising satellite communications business, plus a solid building and construction company.

BAe was a paradoxical mixture of strengths and weakness, of capability and of frustrating ineffectuality. With hindsight, it seems quite likely that when it was created there was insufficient regard for its viability as a competitive organism. We had great technology and a very good outreach to export markets, combined with appalling relations with some customers. We had a lot of wonderful people, yet opinion sampling showed that we also had enormous morale and motivational problems. One middle manager said it well for all of us: 'The company had such great capability and it wasn't adding up to anything. It was really painful. We had product strength, people strength, and a lot of technological and marketing skill. Yet we weren't making the most of it.'

Before we could realise all those strengths, therefore, there was some spring cleaning to do. We had to focus the portfolio around the company's profitable activities. So in early 1993 we adopted a long-term strategy that concentrated all our efforts on defence and aerospace activities. Consequently we exited the corporate jet business, the construction business, some aspects of the property business and the satellite business. In January 1994, we announced the sale of Rover to BMW at an attractive price. We simply could not afford to carry two core businesses, cars and aerospace. At one point Rover was eating up about £2 billion of our banking capacity.

With the shedding of Rover, we arrived at a turning point. At last we could get away from reactive crisis management and begin to conceptualise strategies, and consider who and what we were as a company and what we might be in the future – now that we had a future to talk about.

As we reassessed our identity and our position, British Aerospace's accomplishments, vitality and acumen came more clearly into view. For one thing, we'd actually instituted some major efficiencies that resulted in good productivity improvements. Cycle times on the assembly of wings for the Airbus A320 series were cut from 108 days in 1991 to 59 days at the end of 1994. Regional jets' final assembly times improved dramatically, while labour costs and fixed overhead in the defence business were slashed. These were just some of our infrastructural strengths:

↑ *A staff primed for change* The manpower reduction of 60,000 in a very short period had left us largely with people of our own choice, and that boiled down to a large number of young and energetic people. We had also managed to retain some managers who, earlier at Rover, had had experience with a massive and highly successful total quality management (TQM) programme.

↑ *A wise man at the top* Bob Bauman, our new non-executive chairman, had masterminded the merger of Philadelphia's Smith Kline with Britain's Beecham Group and directed the culture transformation that integrated the two firms. Underneath his cool, laconic style (and the American accent that some of us would jokingly imitate) lie great change management experience and fierce convictions. 'One thing that everyone comes to see as Bob's signature are firmly held views about the sorts of organisations that are going to be successful, those that have the talent for perpetual change,' says former personnel head Rob Meakin. 'Bob had quite a track record, and it was quite clear that he would hold BAe up to a very high set of expectations.'

↑ *A wellspring of innovation* We had great scientific and technological capabilities embedded in various business units, each with strong ties to various universities.

↑ *Financial strength* We had a positive cash flow, a strong order backlog and rising earnings that had placated the investment community. A tower of strength was the Saudi Arabian Al Yamamah II programme for Tornado aircraft, plus in-service training and support, which was signed in January 1993.

⬆ *Faith in the future* Above all, we had a rising belief in our ability.
In 1994 for the first time I had confidence in the contents of the
five-year corporate plan, and no fear that it would, like some of
its predecessors, blow up in my face.

Blips on the radar

These were great strengths, but I was not at all convinced that they
would take us where we needed to go. Events in the marketplace
were signalling the unfolding of a new and harsher environment
for BAe. A real eye-opener came when Boeing, one of our
strongest competitors, revealed a new version of its 737 with better operating characteristics, cheaper running costs, and an
announced price of 30 per cent below the previous 737 model.
When we studied our capacity to emulate this, we found that it was
beyond our reach in the foreseeable future. Meanwhile, Lockheed
had cut the price of its F16 fighter from $27 million a plane to $20
million in three years, and seemed confident of finding a further
$3 million to cut. Similar data from other rivals foretold fierce
price competition in the years ahead, for which we were plainly ill
equipped.

In addition, unfavourable contract terms on leased aircraft
allowed customers to return these aircraft to the manufacturer
without serious penalty. Leasing is essentially an elaborate process
of hire purchase. We had traded aircraft and taken profit on them,
but in reality they were not sold. To undo previously booked 'sales'
of these aircraft, hundreds of them mothballed in dozens of
airstrips around the world, we had to rewrite the balance sheet.

Another dark cloud on the horizon was the halving of US
defence budgets, plus rapid and large-scale rationalisation of the
American defence industry. Mergers involving General Dynamics,
Rockwell, Lockheed, McDonnell Douglas, Martin Marrietta,
Northrop, Grumman and Loral promised to create, thanks to
economies of scale, more powerful rivals than had existed up to
now. 'People didn't realise quite how fast the world was changing,'

said Jerry Wooding, Managing Director, Marketing & Sales. 'The public had less appetite for defence expenditure, so the defence budgets around the world were, and remain, much more difficult to justify. As a consequence, manufacturers have had to go way out into new markets, and they've had to fight a lot harder to win the business in their traditional markets. So we faced enormously increased competition for our traditional overseas markets at a time when our domestic market had down-turned. Just to stand still we had to get better, but better wasn't good enough. We had to be doing what we did a lot better simply to stay competitive.'

The productive capacities of the European aerospace and defence makers far exceeded the demand. There was simply too much capacity in the hands of too many rival producers serving a market half the size of that in the US. There were 10 helicopter and military aircraft contractors (versus five in the US), 11 missile contractors (versus three in the US), 10 armed vehicle makers (versus two in the US), 13 naval shipyards (versus four in the US). When these operations were hit with consolidations, only the fittest players would survive while the weaker fry would have to shut their factories.

There was another element of the external environment that blipped insistently on my radar and further convinced me that a change management initiative was essential. That was the relatively poor performance of BAe shares, when compared to the rest of the stock market. In 1994 we made our first profit in three years and shares had at last climbed to roughly their level at the time of the ill-fated rights offering. However, their relative performance was still lacklustre when set against our sector peers in the FT-SE 100. Our projections of future performance indicated that this gap would widen in the years ahead, in large part because our return on sales was far too low. Meanwhile, the margins of both Rolls-Royce and Boeing were expected to overtake ours. These were but a few of the many indicators that our recovery was far from complete. At our present slow rate of advance, there was a chance that BAe might not survive as an independent entity.

Deciding on change

Why did I think that a culture change was the answer? There were of course many operating and strategic fixes that we could do (and did) to improve our competitive standing and our share price. But when you added all these up, and when you looked at the competitive abilities of rivals, there was a shortfall. I couldn't quantify it. I simply had a gut feeling, a conviction that the underlying reason for our deficiencies lay in the culture of the company.

That summer of 1994, while on holiday in Spain, I decided that the moment of truth had arrived – to launch a radical and uncompromising cultural change push immediately. Furthermore, it looked like I'd have to be the champion of the process. Looking back, my naiveté now seems astounding. Experts make change management sound easy, yet for me this project would prove to be the most difficult task I've ever undertaken. My advice to anyone starting down this road is to recognise that a change programme takes a hell of a lot of hard work, and it is very difficult to deliver on. Change management is not for the faint-hearted. One needs a lot of faith and willpower. Many companies have embarked on big change programmes. Very, very few have actually completed them, or indeed got any appreciable way down the road.

Even with the little I then knew about effecting wide-ranging corporate change, the goal seemed daunting enough. The problem that needed to be addressed could be summed up by a famous quote from Gertrude Stein: 'there was no there there' at BAe. Instead of finding strength through unity of its constituent parts, BAe was a loose federation of independent-minded business units, as had been the case from its birth a dozen years earlier. Says Tom Nicholson, now Operations Director, Military Aircraft & Aerostructures, 'The process of nationalisation had produced no change in our essential character. All that happened was that we changed the signs on vans and doors. Then when Mrs Thatcher decided we would be privatised, we spent more money and changed the signs on the vans again. But we still didn't change in our approach to customers and we didn't work hard at leveraging advantage from each of the strengths within the corporation.'

Whether 'leveraging the advantage from each of the strengths within the corporation' was desirable, or even feasible, could not be easily demonstrated. It was an abstract idea. The enemy was an absence, a void that had to be eliminated – but how? Chris Geoghegan, currently Adviser to the CEO of Airbus Industrie, describes the divisiveness of that time as follows: 'Everyone was intensely focused on their own business units, on what they had to do this week and next week to survive. No one looked over the fence to see the impact of their actions on other business units, or the impact of what someone else was doing would be on them. There was very little dialogue.'

The then Director of Finance and current Vice-Chairman, Richard Lapthorne, remembers: 'We had baronies all over the place.' Mike Wills, Director Financial Control, remembers a paralysing lack of consistency across the businesses: 'We had three manufacturing sites coming from completely different backgrounds. It was absolutely incredible. They did everything differently, everything from personnel practices, recruitment procedures, costing, financial reporting, everything you could think of we did differently.'

There was a high cost to this lack of commonality. The company was poorly disciplined, uncontrolled and uncoordinated – in short, habitually flying in loose formation. Steve Mogford, managing director of Military Aircraft & Aerostructures, observes: 'What we weren't optimising were the possible benefits that would arise from business units taking consistent, common approaches. We weren't optimising the benefits of learning across the organisation; so, for example, technology development was not being applied in a consistent way. There was an element of rivalry between the divisions: some of it was healthy, but some of it was destructive. Clearly, we had not got our corporate act together.' In part this was due to the three-year long climate of survival. When a company is in crisis mode a lot of things get sacrificed. 'We underestimated how much communications had deteriorated among the heads of the divisions during that period of survival,' observes Chris Geoghegan.

To skip ahead of my story, we did get our revenge. British Aerospace launched a centrally directed change programme, called BenchmarkBAe, which achieved – albeit at a slow and deliberate pace – substantial cohesion and synergies across the entire company. Some of its benefits are intangible, and are to be found in new ways that employees think and feel towards themselves and others at work. However, many of the programme's gains have had tangible bottom-line outcomes. Since the company set out on this journey in late 1994, better sales and profits, as well as perceptions of management ability, have propelled the stock price from £4 to £24 in the autumn of 1998. The turnover at the end of 1998 was just short of £9 billion, and the operating profit (before tax and exceptionals) was just a shade over £700 million. And the order book was a fat £28 billion, a 27 per cent improvement over the previous year.

Some of this turnaround is not attributable to the change programme that is the subject of *Vertical Take-Off*, but is due to a wide range of factors such as better strategies, good niche acquisitions, asset disposals, new product introductions, continuous improvement of factory methods and so on. Yet a very large part of the stock price improvement has been the consequence of a culture change programme that fused together previously disparate business units, and thus boosted their ability to create value.

Becoming champions of change

Now let's return to my rather ineffectual efforts in the last half of 1994 to enlist my fellow managing directors as champions of a corporate culture change push. Most people in business assume that the chief executive is the supreme authority, a Caesar who freely directs, commands and controls. I know I did, in my long climb from a pretty obscure beginning in the company, only to find, when I arrived there, that the power of the chief executive is often circumscribed, contingent and conditional. And never was this plainer to me than at this juncture. I knew in my bones that the moment had come to shape BAe into a single coherent entity, yet convincing others in the BAe leadership proved at first to be a Sisyphean task.

I faced two main sorts of objections. First came a number of arguments that reflected the fact that all humans are innately stick-in-the-muds. As I presented my case to senior colleagues, I hardly expected any to stand up and shout hallelujah. People's conservatism, their inertia, their identification with the way things are, make them natural antagonists to change. Any big new initiative in a corporation, or any significant innovation, will come up against this form of resistance. And for good reason, really. In large organisations, most executive energy and effort are directed at fulfilling the basic requirements of the business. Everyone is running flat out. The amount of time and energy left over to consider anything radically new is very small. Consequently, there are always good arguments about the scarcity of resources and of the 'if it ain't broke, don't fix it' type.

But there were also more specific arguments levelled against me by some of my sceptical colleagues:

⬆ Several of the larger business units already had vigorous culture change programmes of their own in place. What was the point of another change programme issuing from headquarters? 'We had all been through change programmes before,' recalls Damien Turner, Managing Director of Consultancy Services at Systems & Services, 'in the sense that we had taken an awful lot of costs out of the business. Lots of words had been bandied round on previous programmes, like "empowerment" and "involvement". But none of them had really operated properly.'

⬆ The business fundamentals were dramatically improving. Both defence and commercial aviation had bounced back vigorously. Consequently, the company was profitable again. The defence order book stood at an all-time high.

⬆ A workforce reduction of 60,000 in the previous two years, plus half a dozen divestitures and all the attendant turmoil, was change enough. What was required was stability, a solid and predictable environment that would motivate people and give them a chance to do their best. Many in the company were on the verge of that demoralising condition called 'change fatigue'.

⬆ Then and now, BAe is involved in dozens of significant partnerships and joint ventures. Any corporate-wide change programme would stop at their gates. Or, if not, there would be uneven application, where the change initiative would be accepted by some partnerships and not others. In fact, it could be argued that BAe's large stable of partnerships was in perfect accord with a holding company at the centre and that therefore my one-company vision was wrong.

⬆ Headquarters simply lacked the moral authority, or the managerial capability, to run this type of project. Divisional pride was inversely related to pride in the centre. Executive Director Mike Turner recalls the mood of those days: 'I remember being out in the divisions and feeling that the guys in the centre had got it completely wrong. The centre had been, in my view, out of control and doing some very silly things. So the strong businesses, like the military aircraft division and Airbus, were going off doing their own things, because they knew what they were doing. And these guys in the centre were making a balls of it.'

To these objections I could have added another: that the record of cultural change in the majority of corporations that had tried it was far from encouraging. Although reliable data was hard to come by, the anecdotal evidence pointed to hundreds, maybe thousands, of programme failures.

Disenchantment with change management was a pervasive theme in the business literature. There were innumerable comments and citations on the pervasive failure of culture change efforts. Here are a couple. In a November/December 1990 *Harvard Business Review* article, 'Why Change Programs Don't Produce Change', three Harvard professors revealed the results of a four-year study at six large corporations. They concluded that: 'The greatest obstacle to revitalization is the idea that it comes about through company-wide change programs, particularly when a corporate staff group such as human resources sponsors them. We call this "the fallacy of programmatic change".' And in the March/April 1995 issue of the same publication, another Harvard professor, John Kotter, had a piece called 'Leading Change: Why Transformation Efforts Fail' in which he noted: 'A few of these corporate change efforts have been very successful. A few have been utter failures. Most fall somewhere in between, with a distinct tilt to the lower end of the scale.'

So what right did I have to think that we could come up with a change management programme that would beat the odds of failure? Of course, we'd be bound to fail if the basic concepts of culture change were flawed. But at face value the concepts seemed to me pretty sound: management can intervene in the underpinnings of culture and get significant transformation, therefore the failures and shortcomings must be the result of poor execution.

I vowed that if we at BAe were to light the lamp of culture change, we would execute flawlessly at every step along the way. We'd go the extra mile to get the principles and the machinery of culture change understood and accepted and we'd never underestimate the power, and deviousness, of resistance, of people's conscious and unconscious opposition and undermining of the change agenda.

Looking over the available sources of wisdom about corporate culture change, one of the things that struck me was a naiveté of expectation. So many companies seemed to think that a modicum of effort and commitment would yield quick returns. At the outset, therefore, we took a view that was very consistent with our basic engineering culture and mindset: to make each part of the change programme demonstrably work before moving on to the next. And if this deliberate approach were to mean that it took BAe twice as long to finish the course, so be it. It became my rule never to make a step change or push the programme forward until we were 90 per cent convinced that those we talked to, and trained and conditioned at each phase, had sincerely bought into the process. That is a high standard, because there is always some residual resistance:

the question at any given time is how deep it runs, and whether it presents an obstacle to further advance.

On one occasion I determined that we were moving too fast and creating insufficient buy-in, so we slowed the programme's advance by six months. Although I was eager for results, I quickly learnt the truth: this had to be a long march. Anyone who thinks that change management can done quickly is in for a big surprise.

One danger that besets change programmes is the curse of superficiality, or too much faith in the power of positive thinking. One day top management says: 'Let's have a change programme.' And after cranking out mission and vision statements, backed with a heavy communications programme, hey presto, they've done it. What are omitted from these narratives are the tensions, ambiguities, conflicts and frustrations that inevitably arise in the implementation phase. These difficulties get swept under the rug, only to return later – most likely in a more virulent form.

I got some of these insights from BAe managers who in former companies had experienced the run-of-the-mill change programme, with the run-of-the-mill lack of consequences. Jim Welch, Military Aircraft & Aerostructures Project Director (Regional Jet), recalls his experience at Ford Motor: 'The change programme literally withered on the vine in less than six months. The slogans were on the office walls and on little plastic cards. But the only time I saw them used was in a discussion with a shop steward who wanted to take a hard line. Then he'd point to the poster on the wall and read "People Are Our Structure" and make some comment that we were not living up to this principle.'

Another characteristic of so many of the corporate change programmes that we studied is their portrayal of the processes of change management as 'soft' stuff, of a different, lesser order than bottom-line, 'hard', nitty-gritty 'real' stuff. This was a prejudicial distinction, which we eschewed. While many aspects of the programme have indeed been attitudinal, motivational, psychological and behavioural, we don't regard them as existing in some separate, 'soft' reality. They are powerful enhancers of productivity and profits, although the way they create value is perhaps a little less tangible than such classic functions as manufacturing, finance or marketing. A distinguishing characteristic of our change effort at BAe had been to be rigorous about measuring cultural shifts and consequent performance gains.

'The Case for Change'

In the eyes of many of BAe's top managers, the lack of a 'burning platform' weakened my argument that change was urgently needed. How could I make them see that the present good times were not symptomatic of the way things would be five years hence? The easier way was to present them with scenarios of likely futures. For this job I turned to one of our top line executives, John Weston, then managing director of Military Aircraft, now my successor as Chief Executive. I seconded him from his regular duties and gave him *carte blanche* to analyse the company from end to end and then report his findings.

With characteristic thoroughness, John documented 'The Case for Change'. His report probed every single part of the business, its macroeconomic environment, its competitive structure, the state of technology and so forth. Time and time again he documented a stark conclusion: our business units' rate of progress and future prospects of performance gains were inadequate, given the emergent threats in the external environment. What's more, even if we took a whip to them to urge them to improve sales and profits and squeeze the cash flow, any conceivable improvement would not change the analysis substantially. At the end of the day, BAe would be trailing and not setting the industry tempo.

Because John Weston was the divisional head of our largest and most profitable business unit, his call to action could not easily be dismissed. If he saw the writing on the wall, so might everyone else. 'We wanted to give them the macroeconomic and geopolitical picture right between the eyes. The paradigm for defence and aerospace markets was changing dramatically, and we had to learn superior skills and ways of reacting,' says Weston.

He also emphasised that BAe didn't have heaps of time to devise a remedy. Five years maybe, certainly not ten. Another point: as with Brutus, the fault lay in ourselves, not in our stars. There were no easy fixes. We had no alternative but culture change. We had to deconstruct the conglomerate that had been BAe's legacy from the day of its privatisation in 1979, and replace it with synchronous, interlocking, synergistic businesses that would enrich one another and thus gain competitive impact for the entire enterprise.

My fellow managing directors neither entirely agreed nor entirely disagreed with my position. 'The most interesting thing about those first meetings were the markedly different visions advanced by each of the five directors,' remembers Rob Meakin, then Head of Personnel, who has since moved to another employer. 'The visions were not hugely different, but each clearly had been coloured by the director's own experiences. Directors who had been grappling with cutting back to the core business found it very difficult to get their minds around the concept of building the business again.'

Reconciling the areas of difference was not easy. To lubricate our interactions we included in our discussions, in addition to Meakin and non-executive chairman Bob Bauman, an American academic and consultant, Warner Burke, who had previously worked on change programmes at British Airways and the BBC. Burke excelled at bringing out areas of conflict and disagreement and then helping us discuss them rationally. As so often happens in business decision making, no one position was incontrovertibly right. There was a contradiction embedded in what I was trying to achieve:

- to retain the positive attributes of decentralisation – including the strong identities and pride of the business units, their focus on discreet technologies and customers
- and yet to infuse the units with the elixir of a cohesive corporate-wide culture.

If I sometimes felt I might be tilting at windmills, I had a Sancho Panza alongside me: the co-author of this book, Colin Price, of

Price Waterhouse, since renamed PricewaterhouseCoopers. Colin Price participated in Benchmark from the earliest days, with a degree of involvement unusual in a management consultant. He did not have a formulaic change management package to sell, just good experience, some of it at Rover.

A large corporate change management programme has so many conceptual headaches, so many wheels within wheels, that a participant-observer like Colin is probably essential – much as I'm loath ever to see a shilling go into any management consultant's pocket. Colin was the right man at the right moment for us. Change management releases complex interpersonal chemistries, which can either help or hinder a programme. Here the chemistries were just right. I've invited Colin Price to write companion chapters to my story of Benchmark: I'll deal with the narrative, he is charged with all the brainy, theoretical stuff about how to do change management, in Chapters 3, 5, 7 and 9.

Only one opportunity

In every corporation there is a quite normal tension between headquarters and the field. The centre has power that is often disproportionate to its knowledge of what is going on in the business. In the case of BAe that tension ran high, which is why some of my fellow senior managers were concerned about the risk of unfavourable reactions by the business units to my ideas for a change programme. As Mike Turner recalls: 'My biggest concern was to prevent a feeling of resentment in the business units – that this was a case of "headquarters knows best". If such a feeling did emerge, then the business units would be hostile to the programme.' I agreed that this was a potential difficulty, but it could be overcome with a programme that was continuously open to input from the business units.

'It was quite obvious,' recalls Meakin, 'that since about 1987 we had been running an organisation which had encouraged the business units to see themselves as separate stand-alone operations finding their own way through life. And it also became obvious that there wasn't a structural way of changing the organisation so that the parts of British Aerospace were brought together. People tended to think about their own individual bits of it and many people had only ever worked for one individual bit of the business.'

My goal was that the change programme would achieve linkages between business units and leave the organisation structure just as it was. Culture change, rather than moving around the pieces of an organisation chart, would be the instrument of unification and corporate muscle building. Still, I would have to be inhuman not to have some moments of self-doubt or frustration at the degree of resistance and the slowness of our progress. Then, I'd often turn to Bob Bauman. I'd pour my heart out and he'd jump in and say: 'Oh yeah, Dick, I recognise that particular situation. Something similar happened to me. Now here's how I'd interpret what's going on, and here's what is likely to happen next.' It was very calming to know that he'd fought some of the same battles and triumphed in the end.

Bob was also generous with his advice to the entire top management team. In the words of Steve Mogford: 'Bob played a key role as the elder statesman. He'd been there and done it before. And he doesn't give the impression of being what he must be, an absolutely rock-hard businessman. He gives the impression of being a coach, a grandfather who wants to look after us and where we are going. He played that role extremely well and I feel Bob's patience and calmness was exactly what we needed when we were grappling with the most difficult issues.'

Benchmark was a blend of authoritarianism and participative management. Initially it had to be a 'Dick Evans Programme', backed by chief executive authority. Soon thereafter it would have to move outwards, gain independence from me, develop its own momentum and affect larger and larger groups of people. In the beginning, just because it was so identified with me, many took the view that it would turn out to be a passing fad, speculating that I'd soon tire of it and we'd go back to business as usual. Eventually, the strength of my commitment did get through to everyone, unequivocally. And the idea that this was a headquarters fad disappeared.

I took a certain risk by identifying myself with this initiative. If it had petered out, due to bad execution or to the strength of the opposition, then I would have had a black eye. Far more importantly, it would have been bad for morale, disappointing a lot of people who'd signed on to the change bandwagon. Failure in a change management programme brings on widespread cynicism, which then reinforces the older patterns and attitudes that were the targets of the change effort in the first place. There would only be this one opportunity, and I was damn well not going to squander it.

Work in progress

This book gives a blow-by-blow account of how BenchmarkBAe was conceived and realised. This is not, however, anywhere close to being a corporate history of this period. It is simply a record of one facet of the recent advance in BAe's fortunes.

The idea of curbing some of the independence of the divisions was not based on some aesthetic idea about organisational elegance. This agenda was the result of a shift in market needs. A supplier who merely sold equipment was increasingly at a disadvantage in defence and aerospace, where the biggest customers had begun to place higher value on a supplier's ability to come up with integrated solutions and complex systems – a change that justified and reinforced Benchmark's one-company focus. Henceforth, 'competitive success in defence and aerospace would depend more and more on a firm's prime contracting and system integration skills,' I told shareholders in the 1995 annual report, because customers now preferred to outsource the responsibility for complete systems solutions, where previously they had done much of that themselves. The more integrated Benchmark made our business units, the better we would ultimately fare in this demanding market environment.

In the years since I wrote those words, BAe has made a number of acquisitions and alliances that furthered the company's qualifications as a prime contractor. Then in early 1999 a unique strategic opportunity arose whereby we could take a giant step forward in this regard. I refer of course to the historic demerger of Marconi Electronics from GEC and into BAe in a £7 billion stock transaction. The colossal strategic advantages to BAe have been amply described to shareholders and acknowledged in the press. Said the *Financial Times* a day or two after the announcement, 'BAe has made itself the only British company likely to win the prime contract for the largest defence programmes, such as aircraft carriers and combat aircraft.'

Some rival defence makers, jockeying for negotiating power in the mergers and partnerships and combinations that will occur as part of the impending global defence rationalisation, claim that we are too powerful. That is not so true on a global reckoning. BAe after the merger will be quite a bit smaller than Boeing and Lockheed Martin. At the time of writing, the likely shape of further defence industry consolidations is unclear – doubtless there will be a first round of major developments later in 1999, with a second round beginning after the millennium.

This merger with one of BAe's best suppliers will yield significant operating economies and synergies. As this book goes to press, many details of the transaction are still being worked on. Only when the two companies are really bonded legally and economically will we take up the issues of cultural integration. I don't think this will be a difficult task, however. Marconi Electronics is a beautifully functioning operation, with first-rate management and people. As I mentioned in the Preface, it has initiated a culture change programme akin to Benchmark.

In the case of other recent acquisitions, such as BAeSema and Siemens Plessey which already had a culture change initiative, we gave them the choice of whether to adopt Benchmark and with what intensity. I suspect that these days it is impossible to merge with a company that does not have an ongoing culture change programme. The dovetailing of two programmes was done with great effect in the case of Siemens Plessey, which was turned around from a loss maker to a very profitable concern and is now one of our business units that is most passionate about Benchmark.

Benchmark is work in progress. It has many more years to run. Culture change is evolutionary. It has to grope its way through uncertainties, inventing itself as it goes along, responding to fresh environments and fresh perceptions and at the same time sustaining credibility with workers and keeping up the momentum of culture transformation. Many hundreds of managers at BAe have been deeply committed to this effort. That it has been successful is in large part due to the many silent heroes in the background who have wrought significant transformations in their behaviour and on their immediate environments – the details of which do not, in most cases, reach my desk.

2
WHO WE ARE AND
WHAT WE STAND FOR

iscussions within the core group of managing directors about the course of change lasted several months. We never really got around to singing perfectly off the same hymn sheet. As Richard Lapthorne observes: 'For a while we floundered around, because there wasn't a common terminology for what we were trying to do. I think everyone thought change meant different things: we were using a common word with different meanings.' But finally there was enough of an agreement among us on the need for change that I had the confidence to take the next step: to expand the debate to the next level of management, and include in our deliberations some three dozen divisional heads and their direct reports. This was to be the pattern throughout the programme, steadily moving the message, the programmes and the support out from the centre towards the perimeter, down from the upper hierarchy to the bedrock of the organisation.

At the first meeting of this larger collection of top managers, I was confronted by the dismaying fact that most of them were strangers to one another. This was fairly symbolic of the very problem I had on the agenda, the need to come together. It was like a gathering of clans, and none too friendly clans at that. Terry Morgan, our current Head of Personnel, was taken aback by the climate of the meeting: 'These were the top 30 or so people in the company and there were people I'd never met, and the majority I was barely acquainted with.' Another participant, Tony Rice, now the BAeAM Group Managing Director (Commercial), had a similar impression: 'Everyone was out of his comfort zone. I am personally intrigued with body language, and these meetings were a good example: everyone used to try and sit against the walls of the room, because there was such deep discomfort around us.'

This was proof of the lacuna at the heart of BAe, the lack of personal ties, mutual support, shared knowledge. To be sure, there were BAe divisions that did indeed know of each other's existence, since there is a fair amount of interdivisional trading of hardware and services across business units, but antagonism and rivalry invariably marred these relationships. If culture is the glue that holds a company together, our glue was clearly five parts water and one part adhesive.

Therefore at the meetings of these larger groups I spoke infrequently, to let others cogitate on the rationale, direction and possibilities for change. I didn't want them to sign on under pressure imposed by the chief. I wanted them instead to draw on their personal experiences and their knowledge of the business, and to consider if an undivided, smoothly meshing company would not be infinitely superior to what they had known up to now.

Their talents and imagination, not mine, would be decisive in realising the corporate change process. My role was at the kick-off and then to be the gadfly and the visible cheerleader on the sidelines. Some of these managers were frustrated with my seemingly laconic approach. They wanted an archetypal leader with all the answers giving orders. Indeed, many were secretly convinced that the debate and the free-form qualities of these meetings (sometimes plodding, sometimes inspired) were really a smoke screen – a prelude to the moment when indeed, like Moses come down from the mountain, I would issue absolute decrees. The refrain I heard then and over the years was: 'Why doesn't the bloody so-and-so just tell us what he wants us to do, and we'll do what he says and get on with it!'

Not that I wasn't tempted: I was. But if I'd given in to temptation, I'd have undermined my own goals. As one BAe manager observed, 'We are very skilled at doing what our superiors would like us to do, yet also skilled at "translating" those messages into something that doesn't really affect us.' This is a good explanation of why chief executive authority is a limited currency in a situation like this one. It is not that people given an order intend to be subversive, it just comes out that way. Unconsciously they 'translate' the command in some way that corrupts its intent.

Another way that people subconsciously attacked our programme was by imagining that it didn't mean what it said, that it was in effect a Trojan horse for the chief executive's diabolical plan to suck power away from the business units and take it unto himself. 'Look, let's cut the crap and get to the hidden agenda' was a not uncommon sentiment at the time. 'We are a very action-oriented group and not very philosophical,' says Steve Mogford, Managing Director of Military Aircraft and Aerostructures. 'We don't feel comfortable unless we are scooting around. And the faster our legs go, the happier we are, effectively. To make time available for contemplation, the slow process of the buy-in, was intensely disturbing. The executives suspected that what fundamentally was happening was that they were being led by the nose to Dick's hidden agenda.'

The hidden agenda theory was just one more manifestation of their insecurity and disorientation and mistrust of this new climate that I was promoting. I denied it and denied it again. Eventually it seemed to die down, leaving room in people's minds to consider the formal intent of Benchmark and their own possibilities for change. Real change can only grow out of the soil on which each individual stands. The perspective from on high – mine, or that reflected in Weston's 'The Case for Change' – could only indicate direction. The applications, the meanings, had to emerge within the individual, from specific situations within the business units.

Though a neophyte as a change architect, I did recognise that there could be no shortcuts. Culture change is a slow, tortuous process, requiring subtle responses and nuanced shifts of emphasis. Early on in the process, I was extremely surprised by the enormous demands on my time and energy. Over the last four years I've spent about a quarter of my time on the change programme. The economic cost to the company and the personal cost are therefore very high. But there is no doubt that in a pretty short timeframe we have achieved phenomenal results. This, of course, justified Benchmark's continuance.

One way to portray a change programme is as the corporation at war with itself: the old self versus the new self that is emerging. Those of us who saw the need for change were nevertheless also snared within the coils of the past. So in the beginning our behaviour was, ineluctably, much as it had been before. There was, for example, the strong hold of a culture that valorised a tough, 'we-know-best' approach. This was very characteristic of our Warton site in Preston, home of military aircraft, where I'd spent most of my working days. We now had to look at Warton's culture, with its veneer of know-it-all, and really question its appropriateness. And other units too. In fact, these units were so unresponsive to each other that Trevor Truman, then Director of Engineering, had a large sign printed up, which he kept in a cupboard and on which was printed in large type the standard answer of a BAe executive to a colleague's suggestion: 'THAT IS A WONDERFUL IDEA BUT WE ARE ALREADY DOING IT.'

We had to face the fact that throughout the company people did not endorse or support cooperative styles of behaviour, such as listening seriously to another's point of view or position. Tom Nicholson does not have good memories of those discussions in the early days. Although the agenda called for change, people's actual conduct was the same old stuff. 'It was dreadful. People didn't listen. They just waited for their turn to talk,' he says. 'It was the worst of all worlds. The guys who made the profit were the guys who clearly could find every reason why everything was OK. It was awful, simply awful. There were just too many people who didn't want to go on the journey.' Observes Peter Hawtin, Corporate Change Manager, 'In those early sessions more than half of the participants thought this initiative would go away, eventually. They expected Dick's attention would become focused on other things.'

There was a lot of wishful thinking of this type. I remember at an early session Ray Wilson, Managing Director of Airbus, saying, and I paraphrase, 'Alright, Mr Evans, I hear what you're saying about this British Aerospace and the one-company focus. But I've just got to tell you that I've only ever worked for one company here and that's Airbus. And until I walked into this room, as far as I was concerned, part of my job was to screw the other people in this room, because they are suppliers to Airbus, maybe even competitors in some minor way – so this one-company stuff is new. What do you want of me? What's this new agenda you are supposed to be setting for me? You say you want teamwork, but how is that going to work?'

Improving the chemistry

Given that sort of baseline, we could only improve the chemistry in these meetings. And we did. The group identified common problems; they gave and got from small acts of sharing. And they plunged deeply into issues of identity, because 'who we are' and 'what we stand for' are the issues at the centre of a corporate culture. So we had to attempt serious institutional and self-examination. If we did not collectively arrive at some pretty robust cultural understandings, we would obviously be unable to set a course for change. Thus with a lot of gritting of teeth and other symptoms of recalcitrance, the upper management group tried open and honest debate on these thorny issues.

A chief executive cannot lead culture change with a big stick. Unless the need for change freely emerges out of honest and open discussion, deep-seated transformation will simply never occur. Since the goal was to change behaviour, we had to deploy group and peer pressure to achieve Benchmark's purpose. So I looked for a balance: neither hurrying the process, nor letting it take too long. Tom Nicholson recalls: 'In the early days Dick never, ever, laid down where we were heading. His stance was, "I'm open-minded on how we get to a better position, but there has to be a better way of doing business than the way we currently do it".'

I don't want to overstate the degree of internal dissonance. Nearly every one of our main lines of business demands complex coordination and teamwork. Most employees were not fundamentally bad team players, it was simply that the teams themselves were not integrated with one another as well as they might be. They did not harmonise. Still, teamwork was at the heart of a number of successes that the company could boast of. For instance, the campaign to sell the FLA super air cargo transporter had been called the 'most effective lobbying campaign the Ministry of Defence had ever seen'. The same could also be said of the rescue of the Eurofighter programme (in which BAe trade unions took a major part in the lobbying push). Then there was the Al Yamamah contract with the Saudi Arabian government. It is impossible to win a mandate on the scale of several billion pounds, covering very sophisticated aircraft like the Tornado, plus scores of diversified and yet integrated support services, without knowing a thing or two about teamwork.

Thus my complaints in this area were relative, not absolute. Relative to the exigencies of the external environment, our company was deficient in cohesion, unity, cross-divisional interactivity. 'Everyone was really intent on their own business unit, what they had to do this week, or next, just to survive. There was very little looking over the fence and seeing what the impacts of our conduct might be on someone else. There was little dialogue,' observes Chris Geoghegan.

'I definitely got the sense that everyone was fed up with the way business units squabbled,' says Locksley Ryan, Communications Director. The big question was how to mobilise that frustration. Our managers might have been immersed in a dysfunctional culture, but they weren't stupid. They invariably knew in theory what should be done for the sake of the company's overall benefit. Nor did the business units entirely lack bridges across their moats. In some functions, like engineering, there were good vehicles for specialists in different business units to share expertise. Part of the message I conveyed was: 'You guys have been vociferous about what a mess this company is – here is your chance to fix it.'

Vision

Our search for identity crystallised around the crafting of a vision statement. Because so many people in corporate life have been exposed to vision statements, it is easy to regard them as intellectually empty propaganda exercises; and in fact many are. But they don't have to be. Done right, the determination of a vision can be a serious act of self-exploration. We at BAe used it both as a mirror to see ourselves and as a way to imagine what we wanted to become. Our vision statement, we decided, should be framed as an overarching goal that everybody in the company could respond to emotionally. The goal we proclaimed was for BAe to be the best in every one of its primary functions, to be the standard by which the world would determine excellence in any activity. The vision statement we eventually nailed to the mast was the following:

> *At British Aerospace we are dedicated to working together, and with our partners, to become the benchmark for our industry, setting the standard for customer satisfaction, technology, financial performance and quality in all we do.*

This declaration was three-quarters hope, one-quarter realism. It belongs to an idealised BAe, not the one we were living in. By most measures of conduct, BAe's headquarters and business units (with some notable exceptions) were at the bottom of the league. But realism was not the point. Vision, says the *Oxford English Dictionary*, is a 'mental concept of a distinct or vivid kind; a highly imaginative scheme or anticipation'. So we packed it full of imagination. We aimed high, because we stood so far down the performance scales. As an expression of our hopes and aspirations to be the best, at this point we baptised the programme BenchmarkBAe.

Vision statements are cryptic. Their value depends on the depth and strengths of their supporting ideas and concepts, the shared understandings that are behind the words. These are some of the underlying aspirations the vision expressed:

↑ World-class quality products and services that set the standard for the industry
↑ Exceptional performance and delivery of products and services to delighted customers
↑ Devotion to teamwork and involvement
↑ Integrity in all our conduct
↑ A winning attitude
↑ Seeking maximum productivity
↑ Mutual trust and respect
↑ Questing for continuous improvement
↑ Measuring our success and our shortcomings
↑ Market leadership across the product line, including preferred solutions provider status with the UK Ministry of Defence
↑ Deep involvement with suppliers from design to final sale
↑ Partnership skills that current and would-be partners acknowledge as adding value
↑ Encouraging City institutions to regard the company as a highly rated blue chip and to show lasting confidence in BAe management.

After the making of a serviceable vision statement, I judged this the moment to expand the reach of the programme and involve more of our top managers. To my surprise, some of the top management team argued that the extension of the programme was premature. Several reasons for delay were given. For instance, the interpretations of the vision were still too fuzzy and needed hammering out. Or there were too many covert oppositionists in the group that still needed to be won over. Or they needed more time to prepare themselves to explain and justify the project to the next level of managers. My dilemma was whether to follow the go-slow advice of the group or to get the show on the road. This inner circle could happily talk for another year at these offsites – generally in good-quality hotels with ample eating and drinking facilities. I had to guard against the whole exercise degenerating into some kind of posh teambuilding.

I went with my instincts and organised the 130 Group, which included all previous participants in our discussion groups, plus the heads and their direct reports of the divisions and some of the joint ventures. Their job was to be the brains trust for the programme's next stage of elaboration. Over the years the group's numbers fluctuated, eventually reaching 170 or so, but throughout this text I shall call it the 130 Group. This congregation, meeting quarterly, would put flesh and bone on to the vision.

Letters to Dick

Early meetings of the 130 Group were pretty stiff and awkward. Once again, candour was in short supply. To urge them to a greater honesty, I insisted that each participant afterwards write me a full and honest reaction to what had gone on in the workshop setting, or about anything related to Benchmark. Thus began the practice of 'Letters to Dick'. At first, many of the 130 Group were distrustful of my promise of confidentiality. But when they saw I was as good as my word, their letters became more communicative. I learnt a great deal from them. They helped me get to know a little about some of the people I'd hardly ever met before. They also clued me in on who the guys were who supported the programme, who didn't, and who were the waverers. Initially the letters' contents were disappointing: far too politically correct and timorous. I complained to the group that I didn't want parrot language, I wanted straight-from-the-shoulder reactions. The trickle of letters eventually became a steady stream. I'd rationed every letter to one page of A4, but soon many ran to two and three pages, a few to ten or twelve pages, sometimes with attachments. As one might imagine, they contained observations that the writer had not felt brave enough to make in front of his peers, for reasons of tact, avoidance of conflict, or because of the damage the comment might to do another person's authority. Some were quite hurtful to the company, but they were important things that needed to be said and would only have been said in the kind of private conduit that I'd created.

'Letters to Dick' was an attempt to deal with one of the trickiest issues in a change programme: allowing forthright criticism of the existing culture in a way that does not attack the company. On the one hand, the programme must encourage a search for truth and give employees the catharsis of letting off steam. On the other hand, it cannot be allowed to bite the hand that feeds us all. Striking the right balance between these polarities is a question of judgement. Inevitably, there will be disagreement on how much criticism should be sanctioned, versus how much deference is owed the company that is meeting its payroll, paying creditors and giving shareholders a dividend.

This said, I think that successful culture change depends on the depth and rigour and specificity of the criticism about the way things have been done in the past: the screwed-up processes, the habits of mind, the irrationalities. 'Letters to Dick' helped to sanction criticism. I was astonished on occasion to read a letter about a subject we'd discussed extensively in the workshop a few days earlier, from someone who'd sat button-lipped throughout. And I'd scratch my head in wonderment at this individual's failure to join in the debate. This was partly explicable by the fear factor – something I consistently underestimated. When I asked people to explain their non-participation, their invariable explanation was that speaking up, being utterly truthful, would be 'an implied criticism of the person I work for'. I replied that open discussions would not work if people held back from speaking their minds, free of the threat of reprisals. The common response was: 'You, Dick, may think that from where you sit. But from where we sit, we think that there will be reprisals against us.' That was a real issue in the early days. It took more than a couple of these workshops to achieve a workable openness.

Now and again I'd get a letter that really gave me a blinding insight of how fear could subvert Benchmark's intent. I once got one telling me that everyone attending from a particular business unit had been instructed by the guy running the division on what to say. My first reaction was incredulity, yet this brave correspondent was right. At this unit they'd go through the agenda in advance of the 130 Group and the guy at the top would decide what position they wanted to take on these topics, whereupon his people would have to toe the party line during the seminar. When I found this out I let that senior manager have a piece of my (fuming) mind.

These letters were also symbolic of my willingness to accept views and perspectives regardless of a person's rank – this in a company where hierarchy had been sacrosanct. They were also useful in correcting weakness in our presentations, communication and workshop content. Because these letters are such an accurate mirror of the evolution of Benchmark, quotations from them are featured at the end of my chapters in *Vertical Take-Off*. I learnt a lot about the guys who responded promptly, those who took a long time, and those who didn't respond at all. Although some letters tended to be sychophantic, these were transparently easy to detect and simply branded the writer as someone not acting in the spirit of authentic and open communication. To a large extent, the early reticence and awkwardness fell away.

But it would not be accurate to say that most of the time we got the level of open discussion and debate that I wanted. What emerged at these workshops were separate realities: one in the open meetings, the other whispered in the corridors and restaurant and bars of the hotel. 'There were times when there were tantrums and heated debates, which was fine,' says Tom Nicholson. 'But a lot of the time people would not say what they meant, and it would spill out outside. So we had this absurd situation where we as a group could reach agreement on positions inside the meetings. But outside the meeting people started saying: "Oh no, that wasn't right." Some of us, me included, got cross that people didn't have the confidence or the courage to say what they felt publicly. Whereupon I became a boring zealot, because I realised that unless we were prepared to speak our mind, whatever other people thought, this programme would not go forward.'

Values

One of the most difficult phases of Benchmark was our discussion of BAe's values. All of us were unprepared for the plunge into symbols and semantics, for the incredibly long debates about the meanings of words, the meanings underneath the meanings. There seemed to be two fundamentally different approaches to our thinking about values. On the one hand, there were managers who objected to the amount of amateur psychology in the air, what they saw as a lot of embarrassing 'gooey', 'treacly' words (as Richard Lapthorne put it). In a different camp were those who understood that psychological matters had to be aired as a prerequisite to knowing what our values might be, and that these issues required a new vocabulary.

These discussions ranged over an entire year. Why did value definition prove so arduous? Couldn't a group of grown, intelligent men and women have done the job in a few hours, an afternoon, a day? Was the BAe culture (present and prospective) really so hard to pin down – the values elusive, intractable, contentious? The answer is yes, which is why it took so much thrashing out. Corporate culture is complex and many-layered, as Colin Price details in the next chapter. Our group was exploring and defining new terrain and being forced to an unprecedented, and often discomforting, level of clarity about identity and culture.

During these debates it was easy for me to identify those who were genuinely contributing to the programme and those who weren't. Those who were opposed, or neutral, I think imagined themselves to be better disguised than in fact they were. Very soon the keen supporters of the programme wanted the resistors taken out and shot at dawn. But I refused to oblige: the non-believers had to be given a fair chance to be won over. We had to respect their intellectual integrity. They could not be hurried.

I don't wish to make it sound as if I were a cool-headed Buddha at these gatherings; I wasn't. I flared up now and again when some comment was made that seemed critical of the programme, or a remark was made that I took to be a criticism of the value of the corporate centre. I do recall that after one of my blow-ups a participant complained in a trembling voice of being treated like a little boy and opining (quite rightly) that if people were torn off a strip when they were merely raising questions about the value of the corporate centre, this programme would have little chance of going forward. I felt really contrite.

Thankfully, I had my ego and impatience in check most of the time. Any flash of temper or display of absolutism would signal the wrong message. The candour and mutual tolerance that marked our discussions would go out of the window and the chances of behaviour change would be diminished. 'Values are just words,' Warner Burke said repeatedly. We had to drill down from values into behaviours. I remember that he offered us an almost Zen-like question: 'How would you know if a person was enacting this or that particular value if you saw it? Tell me, what would you be seeing, what would this person be doing?'

We tried always to keep this point at the forefront of our consciousness. This relentless behavioural focus has been the key to the success of Benchmark. And we're talking not just about the other guy's behaviour, but about our own, mine included. That is why I was happy to get the following comment in a letter from Warner Burke after he'd watched some of our executive meetings: 'Your behaviour is perceived to have changed, and positively. You are seen as definitely committed to this change effort, which I think has surprised some. You have not wavered whatsoever. I don't have to tell you how important this consistency on your part is. You are also perceived to be more relaxed and patient. In fact it may be possible that you are even enjoying life more! On the one hand most want you to "get on with it" and tell them what is going to be. Yet on the other hand there is a recognition of the importance of your allowing debate, and then taking a more measured and careful decision.'

My colleagues all knew that by temperament I'm restless: I love action and deal making. Yet here I was attending more than a score of meetings every year, sitting on my behind, arms folded, much of the time saying nothing, just keeping my hand on the pulse of the group. I attended every hour of every gathering of the 130 Group. 'Initially we questioned Dick's commitment, and the commitment of his team,' recalled Damien Turner. 'But he kept coming to meetings. The fact that Dick was there, all the way through every meeting, convinced us. We were seeing actions rather than hearing words. There are so many events in any company where the announcement is made that "We are going to start now but unfortunately the chairman won't actually be along until later this evening. Hopefully, he will be able to join us for dinner." We knew this programme was serious. We knew that they were going to do all the work that needed to be done.'

I have gone into some detail on this matter to give the reader an idea of how painstaking and relentless the leadership has to be in order to give a change programme credibility and momentum. I suspect that 'Chief Executive fatigue' may have caused some of the reported failures of corporate culture change programmes. It is amazingly hard to push an organisation towards open, broadranging debates on communication, integrity, knowledge sharing, customer focus and so on when the predominant culture is closed to these possibilities. 'The reason behind the problems was the macho culture of British Aerospace senior managers,' says Tony Rice. 'Debate was seen as a sign of weakness. You took a position and tried to get the facts to fit your view. You certainly didn't alter your views. You certainly didn't admit to anything that could be seen as weak rather than strong. Anything that involved a proper debate, a genuine exchange, about "soft issues" like culture was viewed as threatening.'

For Rice and many others too, there was a stark contradiction between what we had been and what we might become: 'The people at the top of the company were the ultimate reflection of the culture, because they had fought their way through. It was a bit like the commanders in the Thirty-Year war during the Middle Ages – when you just attacked everyone you met as you went round Europe. The people who emerged at the end of this historical moment were very tough and very warlike. Similarly the people you met at the top of British Aerospace were the ultimate exemplars of the company's culture. They were focused on task and delivery not on soft issues and debate and psychobabble.'

The values/behaviour debate was confused, often rambling. It raged in brainstorming sessions and subsequently spilled over into hotel corridors and bars. Most of these discussions were really substantive, but I won't deny that there were times when the group sounded like those medieval theologians who argued about how many angels could stand on the head of a pin. 'What is leadership?' 'What do we mean by the word integrity?' 'What does a phrase such as "delighting the customer" mean when you also want to screw him on the price?' 'Does a value like innovation apply to everyone, even the gatekeepers and sweepers?' At one point the group was actively considering about a dozen different values. Eventually, they were boiled them down to five fundamental ones:

Customers
We will delight our customers, both internal and external, by understanding and exceeding their expectations.

People
All BAe people will be encouraged to realise their full potential as valued members of the BAe team.

Partnership
We will strive constantly to be our customers' preferred supplier; our suppliers' preferred customer; a respected partner in our industrial alliances; and a source of pride to our government and local communities.

Innovation and technology
We will encourage a hunger for new ideas, new technologies and new ways of working, to secure sustained competitive advantage for our company.

Performance
We will set targets to be the best, continually measuring, challenging and improving the way we do things both as individuals and as members of our teams.

Note that the values are framed in the future tense. Like our vision statement, these were aspirations – goals of conduct that must someday be realised if the company was to reach for benchmark status in the world. We also wanted these value statements to have a frank and direct emotional appeal – a bit of uplift, the sound of trumpets. And for that reason they are vulnerable to the charge of being simplistic. Anyone can scoff at them, or at any other collection of corporate values. From within BAe I've heard comments like 'they are pretty obvious', that they are 'just catchphrases' or 'does it really matter what the value statement says?' and many other phrasings that say the same thing.

These are easy shots that miss the point, because the worth of a value, its effectiveness as a tool of cultural change, will depend not on linguistic originality but on how deeply it is embedded in the fabric of people's day-to-day conduct. We were not writing poetry, we were trying to run a business. The criterion for a value is that it can be easily communicated and that it is able, with guidance and interpretation, to inspire new conduct and new ways of thinking and interacting.

A value, I'd venture to say, is as good as the energy put into understanding all its dimensions, which is why we created 'Value Teams', one for each value, the members recruited from among the 130 Group. These teams had a common mandate: to validate those behaviours that underpinned each value; to define the practices that would support those behaviours; to find targets and measures to judge progress; to tell us what barriers existed within BAe that inhibited the adoption of the values; and, finally, to recommend concrete actions to embed each value in the everyday life of the company.

In my next chapter we shall discover what the five Value Teams came up with. But first, Colin Price will give the consultant's view on when and how large-scale change management programmes can be successfully undertaken.

Dear Dick

I felt your opening comments were timely and necessary, but I must say that the bluntness of the delivery of the key message did tend to put a dampener on the early part of the session. This needs to be balanced against the optimisation of the team spirit within the group and I would be interested to understand what other feedback you have received around this issue.

***

Dear Dick

The level of waste, untapped skills and talents and the inefficiency of our processes give clear pointers to the enormous opportunity for improvement which exists across our Divisions.

***

Dear Dick

It will come as no surprise to you that the low point of the event for me was how often I had my ear bent about certain 130 Group members failing to 'live the values'. One example particularly horrified me, to the extent that I could scarcely believe it was true. Sadly, the story was later corroborated.

***

Dear Dick

Our employees have lived through many initiatives and unfortunately many of them have not delivered the benefits expected. Therefore it is essential to ensure that any programme we embark on is deliverable and also that it is given clear leadership, visibility, and the results measured.

***

Dear Dick

I was very heartened by your own impassioned introduction which left no one in doubt as to your intention and leadership. I personally believe it gave the harder edge to the whole event which had been lacking previously.

***

Dear Dick

There is a degree of duplication across British Aerospace which is clearly unaffordable and probably inconsistent with achieving a corporate culture. However, as a cautionary note we should not forget that the last time we attempted a company-wide initiative – the overall business architecture – it took forever to define the requirements (which in themselves were 'all things to all men') and another 'time warp' to develop them – by the time all this got done, it was inappropriate to the business.

***

Dear Dick

Finally we have the BAe senior management dragged (kicking and screaming) into committing to cross-company initiatives and thus, by implication, a culture. We need to make sure that the actions that back up the words are politically correct. We all know that some of the presentations were more 'glitz than substance' and we will need regular (and occasionally heavy-handed) reinforcement of our commitment until the remaining doubters (remaining, that is, after the forthcoming management defoliation exercise) finally recognise that this programme is essential and adds value.

***

Dear Dick

Large plenary discussion groups are not the answer as questions seem to be asked only as a means of avoiding embarrassing gaps in the proceedings. Perhaps the introduction of real BAe case studies led by subject experts in small cross-business unit syndicate groups with feedback sessions, would be a good approach.

***

Dear Dick

Although it was brutal, in the cold light of day your opening comments on the choices before us were long overdue. The longer we think that there is a choice with regard to whether we are in this change pro- gramme or not will allow negative sentiments to fester.

***

Dear Dick

The need for enabling tools and techniques to be consistently available and uniformly applied across BAe group is evident. The will at senior management level for the corporate change programme to succeed is tangible. In my view we must move quickly upon implementation of the programme to concentrate minds across the business on the impor- tance of buying into the initiative.

***

Dear Dick

Edward de Bono has said that, in Britain, 'mediocrity is adored'. Overall, I do not think that in the workshop we achieved what the Americans would call a 'class act'. They were, in my view, too much within every- one's comfort zone. They will not give us the big hits we need.

***

Dear Dick

On day two I was not impressed by the 'stress buster'. Maybe I've lost my sense of humour, but frankly I find such things childish. Perhaps some simple physical exercise would be better.

Dear Dick

A chap who was a senior facilitator at SmithKline Beecham tells me that the energy behind their corporate culture change programme has subsided dramatically. This is characterised by fatigue, a degree of apathy, and loss of focus – not unconnected, he says, with the departure of Bob Bauman 18 months ago. My concern is how we can ensure that the initiative that you have started, and the commitments we have made, continue to be sustained in the longer term.

3

WHEN CHANGE MANAGEMENT WORKS – AND WHEN IT DOESN'T

The first thing a management consultant should do when face to face with a new client is to decide if he can help. And, if so, how? Although parallels are sometimes drawn between the consultant and the doctor, I think they are misleading. The doctor has signed the Hippocratic oath and has no choice but to do the diagnostics and apply the remedy. A consultant can, and should, play to his strengths and pick those situations where he might make a difference. If he can't, he should walk away.

In the autumn of 1994 when I first discussed change management with Dick Evans, I wasn't sure what to make of BAe. Here was a company that had just been through a near-death experience, whose ultimate recovery was very much in doubt. Were there, I asked myself, inherent strengths in the company that might be leveraged to springboard a recovery and return it to solid profitability? What might these be? On the other hand, perhaps BAe was just a corporate disaster that had momentarily come up for air, but would soon sink back and drown. I could not make up my mind if the glass was half full or half empty.

This was a company with mind-boggling contradictions. Its bad and good traits were at such extreme poles that it was hard to believe that they coexisted within the same entity. If one could have distilled the well-managed parts of the business and formed a company around them, there was no question that this was a brilliant concern – the equal of a Hewlett-Packard, Intel, Glaxo Wellcome or Lloyds Bank in terms of management prowess. Collectively, the bad parts deserved to be sent to the knacker's yard.

Which was the true BAe? We now know the answer. But at the time there were serious reasons to think that this once-great institution might be on the road to ruin. Were that to happen, not all would be lost – its best assets, like Military Aircraft, would have been sold to others – but the company's demise would have been a real blow to the UK in terms of diminished technology, exports, employment and national standing.

It didn't take me long to decide that whatever the canker at BAe, it was not in the top leadership. It is true that Dick was relatively inexperienced in handling large-scale organisations – a fact that the directors had also pondered after the dismissal of the chairman in 1992. But like them, I decided that he had innate talent, which he and his team had shown in the crisis years of 1992–93: years in which the company escaped bankruptcy thanks only to the incoming cash from the great deal of Dick's career, the multibillion-pound Al Yamamah arms contract with Saudi Arabia, the biggest export order in UK history.

I learnt that Dick and his team had a great deal of depth. Here are some of their attributes:

- ⬆ They had credibility as fire-fighters. They were cool under pressure. The timing and quality of their decisions had won the grudging respect of shareholders.
- ⬆ Management had self-knowledge. This showed in many ways: in the crisis years they were good at coping with rumour, fear, insecurity, uncertainty.
- ⬆ They displayed good tactical and operational knowledge of their businesses.

⬆ They showed dedication to quality products and furthering technical skills.

Above all, even in the worst of times they took the long view. This showed in their priorities. As soon as the avalanche of 1992–93 redundancies ended and cash began to dribble back into its veins, BAe sank a lot of money into new investments in up-to-date facilities and machinery. It vigorously implemented Japanese-style, *kaizen*-based manufacturing methods; it got rid of bloated costs of information technology with a sweeping outsourcing deal.

What finally persuaded me that this company would prevail was not any rational/managerial calculation, but something else. These guys had character, in the old-fashioned sense of 'mental and moral constitution'. Something about their body language, their self-critical qualities of mind and their analytic skills conveyed the right stuff. In the years that followed, I'd see this time and again. They began as complete novices in change management, yet they rarely lacked the ability to grasp issues, break them down and create sophisticated change delivery programmes. In the end, BAe has emerged as the company that in my experience (prejudiced, to be sure) has done culture change the most rigorously and with greatest effect.

In the previous two chapters, Dick Evans began the story of the genesis and the launch of the first payload of Benchmark. My role in this chapter is to take a bird's-eye view of the change management discipline, so that the reader gets a good grasp of the intellectual underpinnings of change programmes in general and of BAe's in particular. Before that, however, I'd like to put this book in perspective. We are not holding up Benchmark as some kind of model for others to follow. In these pages you will not find 'how tos' for the lazy mind. 'You can learn about culture change from other organisations, but you've got to do your own,' observes Tony McCarthy, HR Director, Defence Systems Group.

Managing change

Fifty years ago, change management *per se* did not exist. Its rise and unfolding as a discipline represent a giant stride forward in management knowhow. Nonetheless, the term is often used ambiguously. At one level, change management can mean whatever people want it to mean. It is liberally applied to very limited objectives: for instance, to 'change manage' a better customer interface, or 'change manage' a cycle-time improvement in payables and receivables.

These applications generally do not draw on the skill sets of sweeping corporate change, the kind of big-time change that we address in this book. We're talking massive change, pervasive change, covering a lot of territory and embracing tens of thousands of employees over the course of several years. We're talking change that is designed to yield significant improvements in economic outcomes by transforming an organisation from one state of being to another. And we're talking about an approach that can be applied to any kind of company, large or small, heavy industry or light, manufacturing or service, a people business like banking or a dirty and physical business like mining.

Many, perhaps most, change management initiatives are undertaken in response to developments in markets, technologies and other determinants of competitive success. The speed of exogenous change threatens the competitive abilities of the firm, which is then forced to change in order to survive. Jack Welch, Chairman and CEO of General Electric, put this idea trenchantly: 'I am convinced that if the rate of change inside an institution is less than the rate of change outside, the end is in sight.' Two and three generations ago managers didn't have to contend with the hectic, turbulent and mega-competitive environments we now see everywhere, so they looked at change incrementally and unambitiously. Today, there is one clear imperative imposed on all organisations, Peter Drucker believes. 'Every organization has to build the management of change into its very structure,' he has written in *Managing in a Time of Great Change*.

Change management programmes are vast undertakings, comparable in complexity to filming a movie spectacular like *Lawrence of Arabia* or *Ben Hur*. They are also delicate, in so far as a failure to reach the change objectives is always demoralising and sets off negative chain reactions among employees at all levels. Consequently, in Britain and the US there is no shortage of workers who feel like diving under the table when they hear the term change management. A study of change management efforts in 1991 by consultants Rath and Strong found that 'only one in five companies received an "A" for their efforts'.

The truth is that the specific conditions under which change management is applicable are not widely understood by managers. The all too frequent failures of programmes are the result of insouciant underestimation of the difficulties and gestation time, plus an inability to come to grips with the complexity and subtlety of the undertaking. One company ends up with value slogans that become emptier and emptier with each repetition; another takes the identical slogan and brings it to life as a force for transformation. That is the value of the BAe story in a nutshell, its effectiveness. Many aspects of Benchmark go over ground already well trodden by corporations – a natural result of beginning by benchmarking itself against others – but the thoroughness with which BAe understood and executed culture change is what distinguishes it from so many other corporations that have tried culture change.

Corporate culture

Companies in every industrial and service sector recognise the power of culture. Mike Harper, Chairman and CEO of RJR Nabisco, says it well: 'Culture is a mindset. It's the greatest weapon a CEO has. Change the culture, and you change the world.'

Culture means 'the way we do things around here', a combination of values and beliefs that provide direction and energy to what people do everyday. Although most people don't seem to recognise that they work within a distinct culture, it is everywhere around them: visibly expressed in performance standards, icons, taboos, myths and stories, rituals and the types of relationships that are engendered. Values and beliefs are the deep-seated cultural underpinnings that colour and influence individual and organisational behaviour.

There are many different ways to formulate and describe the ingredients of a culture. In some of the passages that follow, I have drawn on the basic ideas expressed in *Paradox Principles* (Irwin, 1996), by the Price Waterhouse Change Integration Team, of which I was a member and where I learnt much of what I know on this topic. (Our firm merged in 1998 with Coopers & Lybrand, to become PricewaterhouseCoopers. Since most of my work with Benchmark was pre-merger, for convenience the older name is used throughout this book.) In the *Paradox Principles* there is a discussion of the characteristics that define an organisation's culture. I have paraphrased these as follows:

⬆ *Values* These are foundational. They embrace those principles or qualities that are considered worthwhile by the organisation. They may relate to if, and how, people are dedicated to serving customers and clients; their commitment to innovation; their degree of candour and collegiality and/or internal aggression and competition between persons and groups (the latter was a prominent feature of the old BAe culture). Values are more than atmosphere. They attach to almost every element of a business model: customers, employees, shareholders, products, service levels and so on. Values are durable, persisting over time and not always appropriate to competitive circumstances.

⬆ *Beliefs* These too are foundational. They are what the organisation holds to be true and incontrovertible. These are the hypotheses or assumptions that typically go unexamined and unchallenged because they are a view of the world. Beliefs are the source of many notions about competitive advantage and how an organisation should strive against competitors. They are of two kinds: visible and invisible, overt and under the skin of an organisation.

⬆ *Climate* We use this term to synthesise a wide array of behaviours and interactions between employees, and also between employees and customers, suppliers and outsiders. Like values and beliefs, climate is pervasive. It influences, and is influenced by, the physical layout of workplaces, degrees of formality and informality, of consensus building, of individual autonomy and 'right to fail', of acceptable conflict and/or confrontation.

↑ *Norms* These percolate throughout the organisation affecting a wide variety of things, from dress and speech (formal/informal, swearing permissible or not) to collective attitudes to strategic options – such as passionate growth seeking, an always strong balance sheet, expectations of heavy workloads on weekends.

↑ *Symbols* Those icons, legends, rituals and traditions that convey powerful messages about organisational identity and priorities, symbols can be positive or negative, democratic or hierarchic. They can and often do conflict with one another: for example, generous monetary and symbolic compensation of executives will run up against bottom-line considerations. Symbol 'management' involves recognising and adjudicating these conflicts and tensions.

↑ *Philosophy* This is the formal expression of goals, sentiments, policies and methods that employees will consult as a guide to action in day-to-day settings.

These categories are summed up in the illustration below. They are not by any means exhaustive. Corporate culture is as rich and

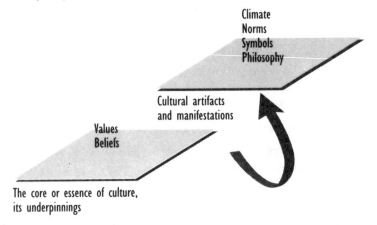

Climate
Norms
Symbols
Philosophy

Cultural artifacts
and manifestations

Values
Beliefs

The core or essence of culture,
its underpinnings

Source: *Paradox Principles*

complex as any other kind of human culture. What the manager needs to understand, however, are those aspects of culture that can be influenced, that are amenable to modification and intervention. That is why we have distilled a complex totality into these six compartments. And of these six, the roots of culture are to be found in the underpinnings of beliefs and values, so it is not surprising that so many culture change programmes are directed towards these and treat the other four as secondary targets.

But all six have a common characteristic and that is the limpet-like tenacity of their hold on the organisation. Without question, the deepest and most intransigent characteristic of an organisation is its culture. Accordingly, it can only be changed slowly and with a great deal of effort. There are, to be sure, other types of management initiatives that cause cultural change – from mergers, to massive reconfiguration of information technology infrastructure, to process reengineering. Indeed, many of these are undertaken because of an awareness of culture issues, as for instance when a company merges with another in other to get an infusion of new blood and new ideas. But to tackle culture head on is the most challenging of all types of sweeping change initiatives.

Corporate cultures vary, far more than most people realise. Differing corporate cultures have both subtle and profound effects on how employees think, interact, communicate and wield power. Corporate culture studies have seen vast advances over the last couple of decades, advances which have drawn from psychology, sociology and anthropology. Yet the dimensions and subtleties of culture remain both vast and ambiguous. One of the pioneers of this field, Edgar Schein, a professor at the Massachusetts Institute of Technology, recently admitted that after a decade of working in this field, 'I keep being surprised by how little I understand of its [culture's] profound influence in situation after situation.'

If one of the world's leading experts can't quite get the message, imagine how much more difficult it is for the average business person to accept and deal with culture! There are other reasons that culture change is so difficult and proceeds so slowly. First, one has to grasp all the elusive attributes of a corporate culture. Second comes the job of nurturing in it new ways of thinking and acting. At BAe the entire organisation, every fibre of it, had to learn how to collaborate; how to become more trusting and open in communications; how to be more flexible on issues of hierarchy and turf; how to wield 'personal' instead of 'positional' power; how to retain the discipline of organisation but allow for fluid boundaries of interaction and knowledge sharing. And it had to do much of this starting from scratch!

While BAe is the first to acknowledge how far it must still travel down the pathway of change, one cannot help but admire the vigour and determination with which it proceeds – as much as one might be shocked at the deteriorated condition of its culture when it set off. An opinion survey in 1995 revealed a culture at BAe that was manifestly in bad shape, as measured by employee perceptions. Leadership, quality, communication, opportunity, satisfying shareholders – four-fifths of the workforce perceived all of these negatively. Even after making allowances for statistical error, for situational bias (where other grievances like pay and working conditions affected responses to these cultural issue questions), the diagnosis was stark: unless there could be a dramatic change in survey outcomes, BAe's competitive position was unlikely to improve.

As we said a moment ago, all culture is deeply rooted – the bad and the good. This is why culture change holds such high promise of adding value. But it is not a tool for all seasons, so let us now examine those conditions under which culture change can add value, by first looking at those four conditions when culture change is not advisable:

- ⬆ when there is no economic logic, or future, for the business;
- ⬆ if the sources of competitive advantage are not relatively clear;
- ⬆ if the existing culture is not out of synch with the strategy;
- ⬆ if the company lacks a capable and committed leadership team.

Let's take each of these points in turn.

Economic logic

Culture change is no panacea. It is not for companies where the business lacks fundamental economic logic. The most brilliantly conceived and executed culture change programme will be a waste of time and money if you are in the buggy whip business at the time that the steam engine is taking over transportation. Then culture is irrelevant. Or say that the company's fundamental *raison d'être* is played out, like Hanson Industries which thrived for a while by acquiring cheap corporate assets and then squeezing a lot of cash out of them. When that formula no longer worked, Hanson awoke to the fact that it had all the disadvantages of the conglomerate form, which culture manipulation could never have changed, and quite sensibly demerged.

In the dark days of 1992 and 1993, one wondered if BAe was not a case like Hanson, something to be fed to the corporate scrapyard. There were several factors supporting this point of view. Aside from its conglomerate features, BAe's biggest and most profitable division faced the end of the Cold War, shrinking defence budgets around the world and powerful US players, busy merging with one another to become yet more powerful. Dick Evans was pretty clear-headed about these facts, saw opportunity where others might have been tempted to despondency. The shape of this opportunity lay in shedding the attributes of a conglomerate and then using culture change as the force that would weld the business units into a coherent and focused entity. In this way, he reasoned, BAe's enhanced competitiveness would lead to a greater share of shrinking markets.

Previous procurement policies by customers, notably the UK's Ministry of Defence, had stressed the purchase of parts or subassemblies, which the customer would then integrate with other parts from other suppliers. One could therefore argue the organisational benefit of highly autonomous divisions, even if they sometimes got in each other way in the customer's offices. But in recent times, BAe's customers have increasingly moved away from buying bits towards larger purchases of nearly assembled manufactured units and systems. Under these circumstances, any logic supporting strong divisional autonomy evaporated. A consummate salesman, Evans sensed the need to do something about the new rules of order getting, hence his drive for greater corporate unity. Although he did not in fact initiate a change programme until the autumn of 1994, in retrospect it seems to me that all his previous strategic fixes ineluctably led him to try and forge BAe into a single unit, a cohesive and thus greater power than its constituent parts.

This quest for synthesis, for pulling out the maximum benefits possible in a large grouping of diverse businesses, is an enduring challenge in most big corporations. Pilkington's, for example, has been strenuously working towards this goal, as part of a massive effort to create annual savings in the range of a quarter of a billion pounds. In the process, senior management is transforming the glass maker from a federation of semi-autonomous, country-based businesses into a single, global group. To this end, the company has closed a number of national head offices around the world, each of which had a powerful bureaucracy, indigenous identity and chain of command.

But this popular goal among CEOs of forging unity, releasing synergy, achieving the shared strength of the multidivisional corporation often turns out to be a snare and a delusion; sometimes, in fact, shareholders are better off with disaggregation. There is an occupational bias at the top of large diverse corporations to resist the logic of break-up, to refuse to look at the benefits of releasing subsidiaries from bondage and letting them go off to an independent existence. It is often a close call as to which is the proper path, and it was certainly a difficult dilemma for Dick Evans in 1994. Even after the disposal of the car, property, construction and satellite businesses, there was a rationale for further divestiture of the aerospace and defence units into vehicles for public investment. Two factors argued against this course. One, defence is perforce a very 'political' industry in which scale is an important quality. As independent entities, the subsidiaries might have faced tough going and therefore shareholders might not have ended up better off. Two, there was the promise (albeit an ambiguous one) of adopting culture change.

Sources of sustainable competitive advantage

If a company's sources of competitive advantage are not clear, then it is too soon to address issues of culture change. Without a compelling strategy for the business, culture change is of doubtful value – because to align culture with the forces that generate success you first have to know what those forces are. Thus an understanding of today's sources of sustained competitive advantage is the bedrock of any good change strategy.

The need for an all-round competitive 'fitness' in the face of uncertainty has fuelled many change management projects. Royal Dutch/Shell, for example, boasted dominant and highly profitable operations in the big oil sector, but nonetheless management felt that it needed greater preparedness for a variety of unforeseeable threats and opportunities. A change programme was the consequence. BAe was not like the Shell case, nor did it face a 'burning platform' kind of crisis.

But on balance there was enough momentum, backed by fundamental competencies, to justify BAe's investment in change. This is in contrast to many companies suffering from strategic myopia, which put the cart before the horse, opting for change initiatives instead of confronting and dealing with their competitive inadequacies. This can be a very high-risk approach. The CEO of a very large oil company some years ago launched an enormous and highly publicised cultural change initiative. It was perceived as a resounding failure and ultimately contributed to his dismissal.

Misalignment of culture and strategy

Culture change is only justified by an identifiable cultural problem. So if culture is not out of line with strategy, then no intervention is necessary. There are many companies whose strategy is right, and whose culture is right, but the operational performance is poor. In this case, it is the latter that has to be addressed. This, it might be argued, is just common sense. True enough. But it often happens that companies don't see it that way – in part because they misidentify culture – and go on to apply culture change techniques to operational issues. Here again we find another explanation of why the aggregate statistics show that many culture change programmes fail.

An organisation may possess a strong culture but one that is wrong for the business; for instance, a people-oriented culture won't work in a business where success depends on the lowest possible end price, with no innovation, no customer service, *nada*. Then the corporation will strive always to achieve rock-bottom labour costs and benefits and invest little in working conditions, factory safety, hygiene or morale factors. So managers need to ask: 'Do we have a strong or a weak culture and, secondly, does our culture (strong or weak) fit with the strategy?' The ideal is to have a strong culture with a good fit to strategy.

There is a solecism in a lot of management writing that equates success with strong culture: we are inclined to think that high-growth and highly profitable firms like Intel, Microsoft, Nike, Coca-Cola and Glaxo Wellcome have great cultures. Maybe they do and maybe they don't. There is not 100 per cent correlation. Success can be largely independent of culture. A measure of strong culture is the degree of cohesion, the binding strength of a group's norms of behaviour and thinking. The strength of a culture lies in both manifest and unseen assumptions. Where deep, taken-for-granted roles and conduct are widely shared, and both control people and release their creativity, there is likely to be a strong culture.

Many companies have significant problems but culture is not one of them. Technology changes, demand dries up, banks pull the plug on credit, governments impose new regulations and so forth. Immediate survival issues cannot be fixed via cultural dimensions, if only because deep and pervasive culture change is achievable too slowly to be a coping mechanism. Fortunately, by the mid-1990s BAe had got over its crisis of survival. By 1994 it had a breathing space and thus could address the lamentable fit between culture and strategy.

Its fundamental problem of too much divisional autonomy is quite common in large firms. Over time, organisations veer towards centralisation and then a decade later veer back again to decentralisation, and then reverse direction again and strive to be more centralised. A case in point is Allied Signal in the US. Roughly a decade ago this company had more than 50 separate divisional fiefdoms in automotive products, engineered materials and aerospace. Many of these had been acquired via acquisitions to fuel growth. Larry Bossidy moved from US General Electric to assume the top spot in 1991, and his avowed mission was to end a 'strange marriage of disparate companies that no one had really tried to weld together'.

Bossidy did a magnificent welding job that powered impressive revenue growth and quantum profit improvements. One way he achieved cultural change was the establishment of values, which were communicated and taught down through the organisation. Every year Bossidy makes a slight revision to the value statement, in the light of changing conditions, but at the heart of it is the drive to forge a single company in which divisions act in concert.

The matrix overleaf summarises these points. On the left-hand side the strength or weakness of a culture is measured, that is to say its internal unity, cohesion, shared values etc. Organisations will range from high to medium or low on this scale. On the base of the matrix we measure the culture's degree of 'fit' with the corporate strategy and the consequences this holds for a corporate change effort. The ideal that should be striven for is to arrive at the upper right-hand box: where there is a strong culture that has a high fit with strategy.

Leadership

Unquestionably, leadership drives culture change. The word leader conjures up a man in uniform astride a charger, sword in the air; a Wellington, a Custer. Such a primitive form of leadership is

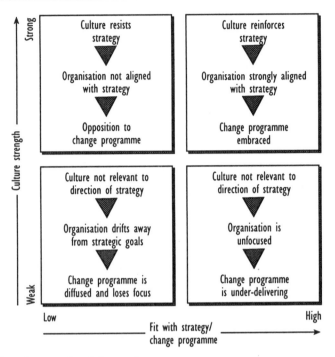

not what is required in a change management programme, quite the opposite. What is essential is a leader who creates greater synergy, cohesion, focus, who enhances social organisation. Leaders influence culture through the neurons of the organisation. They do not bark orders: they create connections and relationships that spur efficiency, innovation and other intended behaviours and attitude.

Many companies have gone through a rite of passage similar to BAe, snatching victory from the jaws of defeat. For instance, the engine maker Rolls-Royce was in a trough of despond following the 1991 loss of British Airways' engines business in the Boeing 777. BA's switch to GE was a body blow. 'In the big engine chess game, Rolls-Royce has just lost its queen,' said one analyst at the time. But it seems to have been a seminal moment: thenceforth the engine maker broadened its product lines, reduced costs and undertook a culture change that powered massive gains in market share.

In a similar vein, General Electric's Jack Welch devoted the first years of his CEO-ship to a radical cost-cutting and downsizing programme, including drastic shrinkage of the corporate centre. The success of this endeavour acted as a platform for one of the most ambitious and successful corporate change projects on record. Yet even Welch faced major tests to his leadership from powerful executives who refused to sign up to the programme, yet were major contributors to GE's profit. Faced with this dilemma, Welch did not hesitate: the cultural foot-draggers were told to leave the company. The integrity of his leadership, as well as the programme, was at stake.

Change management initiatives are too vulnerable to be encumbered with recalcitrance or neutrality. They need lots of nurture and leadership. The *sine qua non* of successful change management is the stimulation of leadership qualities at all levels of the organisation. Later in this book we shall describe the extensive efforts made under Benchmark to promote and disseminate both the psychological and operational facets of leadership. Of the many change programmes I've witnessed at close hand, none has had the strong leadership and commitment demonstrated by BAe.

Inadequate leadership at the top is the most common source of change programme failure. The seeds of failure are often laid in the beginning, when top managers cop out on their number one responsibility, rigorously and candidly to define the present state that needs changing. It is excruciatingly difficult to be honest about the company's shortcomings and its skill and attitude deficits. Above all, the leaders must not shirk the truth. They *must* acknowledge that they more than any other factor (more than unions, more than 'industry conditions') are part of the problem; they, their behaviours and modes of thinking, are what created the situation that must be overthrown by the change project. Second, they must not underestimate the time and energy and resources that are needed (including significant amounts of top management availability that must be stolen from private time, or from day-to-day operations). So leaders have to pace themselves. At the peak of programme activity they must be prepared to spend perhaps as much as half their time on this project. And during programme planning and 'normal' execution and follow-up, the demands will still be high, running to maybe a third of diary time. My third point is that leaders have to think boldly and imaginatively. They must tolerate the risk that their attempts at behavioural change may fail. Timidity in goal setting, pessimism about people's potential for adapting to the change order or cautious politicking will all doom the change process.

I don't think that at the outset BAe had all of these three qualities in abundance. It had a sufficiency. Moreover, Dick Evans and his team did recognise the need to nurture and grow them as they went along. And they also understood the crucial fact that change management is fundamentally unlike anything else in the managerial environment, that previous education and experience are no guide to the kind of demands and stresses that change management creates. The way, the path, is learning by doing.

'I've experienced several change programmes in other companies. The difference about Benchmark that sets it aside from the others is the amount of time and effort that has been spent by the leaders – making their mark and giving it their stamp. There has not been what I've seen elsewhere, delegating change management to a set of willing champions. Very soon those champions hit a wall because they don't get the support they think they are entitled to,' says Terry Morgan.

Dick Evans and I did not always see eye to eye. And one area where I kept giving the same advice was equally met with the same resistance from him. In early discussions of the change programme agenda, both the American consultant Warner Burke and I warned him that he had to be prepared for a lot of blood on the floor of the executive suite. Warner and I argued that the evidence from the many hundreds of companies that had tried sweeping culture change – all the post mortem picking over their carcasses for reasons – showed one thing: the greatest resistance to change emerges at the top of the corporation. It is the old wine bottle story: the constriction is in the neck of the bottle, not below. When both Warner and I predicted that to make the programme successful he'd have to purge about a third of the senior management group

Dick looked like we'd kicked him in the stomach, such were his surprise and dismay.

'Why so many?' he asked.

'Because that is the degree of the resistance in the upper executive group,' we replied. 'That is what Jack Welch of GE recognised.'

'Well, I'd like to be absolutely certain that it's necessary.'

'It is. At least 30 per cent of the management, you will find, are a major obstruction who will create a massive credibility problem,' Warner and I replied.

Instead of having a night of the long knives, Dick felt that if the executive group was given enough time and persuasion, they would sign on wholeheartedly. 'Where Warner and you got it wrong,' he has since said to me, 'is that you didn't (and I didn't) at the time realise that our group of senior managers were much more open to change than a normal population. We had shed 60,000 people in the space of two and a half years. Even if we'd got that process half right (in who we wanted to retain and who we wanted to let go), the chances were that a large proportion of the senior management who would be potential obstacles had left the company.'

In the event, fewer people in the upper echelons were made redundant than I had predicted. And, of course, some elected to quit, simply repelled by what the culture had become. Given the degree of change that has been achieved, and the relatively small number of holdouts that exist, I am happy to do what I rarely do: admit that my professional opinion was wrong!

4

THE VALUE TEAMS
GO TO WORK

'Progress is the mother of problems,' said Chesterton. Following the launch of Benchmark, we confronted the problem of actually doing something to move the body of the company towards its goal. The initial brainstorming was over, the overture was finished. Now we had to make our vision real.

As so often in the evolution of Benchmark, we asked senior operating management to shoulder the burden and take us to the next stage. We asked them to create five Value Teams – customers, people, partnership, innovation and technology, and performance. The Value Teams consisted of members of the 130 Group, each led by the managing director of a significant business unit, plus a coach, also drawn from the upper levels (for a while I was the coach of the Customer Value Team). Each participant in the 130 Group had a role in a Value Team, and each was expected to contribute significantly to the effort. Most Value Team members put in one or two days a week over a three- to six-month period. They made many outreach visits to other corporations and to BAe facilities; they formed special taskforces, they did opinion surveys of customers and employees, and they brought in facilitators and consultants.

But what gave these quasi-think tanks really high octane was the fact that their staff work was in the hands of the best and the brightest young managers recruited from business units for a year's service. 'We got energy from them and a different perspective from the great and the good who were driving the programme, who in reality were not those at the coalface of the company,' observes Mike Wills, Finance Director of Aerostructures, who served on a Value Team.

One of the central questions that each Value Team addressed was this: how would they determine if and when a value was actually embedded in the company? What behaviours, attitudes and body language would give the signal that real change had occurred? Furthermore, what aspects of this embedding process could be measured and thus provide a map of progress along the road? Another mission of the Value Teams was to identify the key barriers and roadblocks to Benchmark's realisation.

What we didn't want was for them to use the all-purpose excuse 'Oh, it's the BAe culture' whenever they hit resistance. We wanted hard-edged observations. We asked the teams to give us details on each barrier they encountered. We wanted to know about, for example, performance measures that reinforced a certain kind of behaviour, or leadership practices that gave contrarian or mixed signals, or operating and information systems designed to support the conglomerate-style organisation, or reporting requirements that encouraged obfuscation. Once identified, all these could actually be changed. Additionally, we asked each Value Team to check its work against the other teams', in case there were conflicts or overlaps, or areas where they might help one another. The total investment was considerable but, as with all aspects of Benchmark, we felt that there was no point doing it on the cheap, since that in and of itself would convey the wrong message, besides risking a poor rate of progress.

The Value Teams marked a devolution of power, a transmission of authority away from the senior directors of the company. Their composition – a melange of top people from different business units – also represented a symbolic step towards the one-company goal. The Value Teams' use of younger managers, working side by side with those of much higher rank, demonstrated that one didn't have to have seniority to influence the company's future direction. Previously, BAe had been pretty rigidly divided into high- and low-caste managers.

One of the leaders of a Value Team, Tom Nicholson, has this to say about the experience: 'It was enjoyable, but it was scary. We were bringing together groups of people from across the business, people who had known about each other for a long time, by reputation, by folklore. During the couple of years we worked together we certainly found a lot of these people weren't like their reputations. They were good people, they did have good ideas, things to offer and contribute. Yet very often in the early days they lacked the confidence to offer some really good contribution for fear of being unable to sell it back home, as it were, in the business unit. But by the end of the two years several of the members felt and behaved as a corporate group. They wanted the best for the company. And they developed a pretty low tolerance for being told: "Well, we don't do it that way in the business unit." They'd risen above the business unit's restrictions and constraints.'

But this 'rising above' the parochial sensibilities of the business units took some time. Initially, some participants in the Value Teams felt that local interests kept creeping into the discussions and undermining the focus that should be on the company as a whole. Slowly these traits were worn down and abandoned, and eventually the Value Teams developed their own pan-BAe *esprit de corps*. Says Mike Wills: 'It dawned on us that we'd been given a very significant mission, which had to produce deliverables. We all felt loyalty to the Value Team, and wanted to do a good job – that was very significant in building commitment to the total programme.'

One of the chief missions of the Value Teams was to address the issues of behaviour, attitude, practice and culture that impeded our efficacy, in other words the 'blockers'. Without a very forthright picture of the existing blockers we would never summon the will, or the right direction for culture change. I was given a lot of information from other companies on the severity of blockers. In a major recent study of 500 organisations in 14 different countries, Price Waterhouse came up with some very good findings on a dozen of the main barriers to change. These, in descending order of significance, were:

1   Competing resource priorities (always a whinge at BAe)
2   Need for change poorly explained
3   Employee opposition
4   Lack of middle management support
5   Insufficient change management skills
6   Initiative fatigue
7   Inadequate communications
8   Unrealistic timetables for the change project
9   Inappropriate leadership at the top
10 Insufficient training and coaching
11 Lack of clarity of vision and objectives
12 Bottom-line benefits not understood

The list's length is sobering, because it shows how many factors of change have to be done right for each of the blockers to be neutralised. Many of the factors listed above, the report pointed out, related to commitment, while others related to skill issues. The most powerful were the people-related barriers, such as active opposition, inadequate involvement, lack of senior management support. The weaker barriers were about skill deficits. 'It would seem that focusing on the commitment-related areas should yield benefits on twice as many programmes as with skill issues,' said the report.

Intuitively we understood this at BAe: that if you could generate the commitment first, the actual processes and programmatic things would develop spontaneously. But before it was possible to generate authentic commitment the blockers had to be addressed: all we did wrong, all the subterfuges and delusions and mistargeted efforts with suppliers, customers, colleagues, partners.

After they had nailed down the blockers, the Value Teams had the mandate to look beyond things *in situ* and to the best standards of practice anywhere in the world. Insistently, they targeted and re-targeted the questions: 1) What is benchmark in this or that area of performance? 2) What will it take for BAe to emulate that benchmark? We wanted them to deliver all the meanings of a value, in great depth, and we wanted them to be concrete and to indicate the kind of actions that would follow out of the values.

After six months of investigation and inquiry, the Value Teams reported their findings and recommendations to the 130 Group. What follows is a report on each team's methods, dilemmas and discoveries.

Customer issues

In most aspects of customer relations, BAe was about as far from being a benchmark as anyone could imagine. But for the technical quality of many products, the case against us would have been completely damning. When customers complained, both intra-BAe customers and the external revenue producers, BAe people had a habit of shrugging them off. Although some three-quarters of total company revenues stemmed from repeat business and it cost five times more to win a new customer than to retain an existing one, customers were not treated with tender loving care at BAe; quite the opposite. 'It was easy to prove to the BAe people that they were terrible at customer relations, just awful,' says Bob Bauman. 'They knew it. They didn't have to be told.' Jerry Wooding, Managing Director, Marketing & Sales says: 'We did some surveys which showed that there were only one or two areas where there was more than a molecule of real customer satisfaction. In most of our markets we poked along and achieved the minimum standard, along with a lot of dissatisfaction.'

We learned, to our chagrin, that we had a reputation for being incredibly unresponsive towards our number one customer, the UK Ministry of Defence. We discovered this unpleasant truth when we sat down with them to discuss the relationship. Arrogant was the word they used to describe our attitude. It was quite a shock to hear that from them, so we asked for examples. They shot back, 'One, you are great at telling us you are always right and we are always wrong. Two, it would be a lot better if you put things to rights on programmes you currently have, before you launched a marketing effort into selling us something else. You'd be a lot more effective and believable if what you were working on today was actually right, and it isn't. Fix that and then come and talk to us about what you want to sell us tomorrow.' More often than not, they told us, when they called up and said there was a problem, BAe people replied that there would not be a problem, if only they (nitwits were implied by tone of voice) followed the correct procedures.

Here's an example of what the RAF might often have to do to attract our attention. First, they'd contact one of our engineers, only to be told right off that this was not a design defect, not a problem inherent with the product: the RAF was simply not following the service manual. 'Read the manual, do what it says and the problem will disappear.' Only after they badgered us time and again did we get it through our heads that they had been following the procedures correctly, whereupon, very ponderously, we'd concede: 'Well, actually you might have a point.'

Clearly, we had a culture that was out of touch with reality. Many of our engineers seemed incapable, when the Ministry of Defence made contact with us, to respond instinctively with: 'If you say you have a problem we believe you and we'll be right down there to look at it.' They imagined that it was their job to keep the customer in his place.

Unhappy customers talk, they talk a lot. They are three times as likely to complain to others about some unsatisfying experience than to express satisfaction over something that went well. Then and now, BAe only had a handful of customers: 20 really big ones accounting for some 80 per cent of volume. What's more, many of these were situated outside the UK and would hardly be swayed by an appeal to Buy British.

Here is the kind of feedback we got from surveys of customers. 'We are never surprised when something goes wrong with BAe,' said one senior executive at the UK Ministry of Defence, who continued, 'We expect other companies to perform beyond our expectations, and many do. But BAe generally performs below our expectations.' Another Ministry of Defence source said: 'Senior management is always shooting from the hip, so they'd promise something by the end of the next week. But when we speak to the junior management it turns out there is no way these promises can be kept.'

The Customer Value Team responded to such downbeat assessments by immediately asking the big question: What would it take to reverse our standing with customers and be benchmark in this area? The answer, they decided, was to truly put the customer at the centre of our business. BAe had to become a customer-focused business that believes, in every organisational neuron, that it is the customer who decides the quality and success of our business. In addition, it would be an organisation where every employee exhibits awareness and understanding of the changing needs, opinions and concerns of the customer. And for this to happen, of course, it would have to create an accurate profile of exactly who the customer might be. Is the customer the UK Ministry of Defence, the procurement arm of the RAF, the flyer of the aircraft, the maintenance people? And if all of the above, how do we bring each one into appropriate focus?

Fortunately, there were some areas of the company where we had a decent track record at meeting customer desires. The Rapier 2000 programme from the Dynamics Division and the Military Aircraft Division's (MAD) work with the Ministry of Defence on the Harrier received high marks in our customer survey. We studied these to see what practices could be transmitted to other parts of the organisation. Then we deconstructed a major internal customer relationship: between commercial aircraft maker Avro (RJ) and Aerostructures at its Filton facility – again looking for best-practice tips and tools.

Customer relations are complex in the defence business. It is not like selling soap or shoes. The actual time from doing the groundwork, to bidding, then executing, then after-sales service and maintenance occurs over many years. Over the life of a contract, which will typically run in excess of 10 or 15 years, the actual ingredients of what is being manufactured will often change, because the customer demands it for any reason from technology to politics. What is more, over these many years there will be a succession of new personalities on the other side of the table. There are very likely to be changes in how the customer is organised.

When analysing issues, it would have been easy for the Customer Value Team to take the position that our industry is unique in its customer interface and consequently there was nothing that could be learnt from non-defence companies. That had been a predominant outlook in years past. But now we had to broaden our minds and seek new possibilities if we seriously aimed to be benchmark. So the Value Team visited seven companies outside the aerospace industry which were recognised as good at customer service. It was an eye-opener. What we learnt was that really excellent performers towards customers showed consistent behaviours across their organisations: they had great mapping and accountability; they understood customers' agendas, and also their culture and processes. All of these attributes could be summed up in a refinement of our original customer value statement to know, measure, understand and delight the customer.

Ten years ago customer satisfaction was an adequate goal; no longer. Customers need to be more than satisfied if they are going to regularly give repeat business in the present market. There has been a tremendous spread of defence and aeronautics knowhow across the globe and many countries that were quite primitive in this area a decade ago are now strong contenders. Standards are higher, so is the competitive rigour. Meanwhile, there has been a structural shift away from bits of hardware towards total systems. The decisive competitive advantage is less and less in the black box and more and more based on superior service and the ability to understand and respond holistically to customer needs, present and future.

The Customer Value Team tried to imagine what kind of an experience it is to have BAe as a supplier. They studied customers' needs, culture, organisation, processes and criteria for satisfaction.

After credibly demonstrating to our customers that we were determined to change, the team invited customers to share their perceptions and insights in workshop and brainstorming sessions. Up to then, BAe had known very little about customer mapping. Now it learnt the approaches and techniques. Many of the subsequent improvements in customer relations we owe to the work that the team did on mirroring customer organisations and 'marking' customer personnel for appropriate coverage.

In many respects Benchmark was cathartic: it released a lot of pent-up energy and direction. Jerry Wooding was part of a pilot team that did a couple of projects about mapping a customer contact plan for the Harrier. 'These guys said, "This is excellent stuff! We must have much more of this." We are now in a position to understand the orchestration of our resources with the customer: because we are putting too little effort in some areas and too much in others. It was a superb and really eye-opening project.'

Performance issues

By definition, the very heart of Benchmark is measurement: not for its own sake, but because of the power of comparative data to spur change. A benchmark creates a bogey for the course against which the player judges his skill, which made it additionally appealing to a life-long golfer like myself. In business, how things are measured determines what gets done, how it gets done, by whom and with what outcomes. Measurement creates reality. To learn how we're doing, where we're going and what shape we'll be in when we arrive, we measure. But there are measurements and measurements. An organisation can readily develop measures that appear to describe an important reality, but in the end don't. When people use unreliable measures to guide their decisions and behaviour, they are acting under the influence of an illusion. That, in a nutshell, was the issue addressed by the Performance Value Team. BAe's abundant stream of existing measures weren't showing us the real picture; if they had, the company would have never got into the mess that it did in 1991–92.

Quite aside from their flaws as accounting tools, many of the measures we used were destructive because they did not spur BAe people to the kind of conduct that improved efficiency. Even measures that were used successfully by other companies, such as the celebrated EFQM Framework (European Federation for Quality Management), when applied by some BAe business units, didn't bite deep into the operations. EFQM is the work of a non-profit, corporate-sponsored group that supports a standard for measuring business performance across a wide spectrum of activities. Alas, BAe's EFQM scores were not good. To win a coveted EFQM award, an institution has to rack up a total of some 750 points or more. BAe's business unit scores ranged from 250 to 350, seriously behind our expectations for improvement. Meanwhile, hundreds of different companies across Europe were doing a lot better than us at improving their EFQM record.

To stop being a laggard and become a benchmark standard bearer, BAe had to make a quantum leap up the learning curve. To do this we would have to deploy all the powers of Benchmark, and also install measures that drove performance along the key vectors of productivity and efficiency. Furthermore, we'd have to stop the practice of permitting business units to go their own way in selecting performance measures. Even those that had adopted the EFQM framework applied it in idiosyncratic ways. Diverse and irreconcilable performance measures simply reinforced divisional remoteness from the centre and isolation from other divisions. To be a single-focus company we obviously had to use the same performance criteria.

Since I took over as CEO, many of the company's business units had adopted somewhat better measures than previously, especially those focused on higher cash generation – thanks mostly to the efforts of our then Finance Director, Richard Lapthorne. But a hugely accelerated cash flow was just a start. In order to adopt and then extend world-class performance measures into the total life of the company, the Performance Value Team urged the following types of behaviours:

↑ Adopt best practices from within or outside the industry.
↑ Use rigorous performance measures, milestones, deadline setting.
↑ Create demanding targets that are continually measured and monitored against performance.
↑ Set key performance indicators for all managers and communicate these broadly.
↑ Initiate ambitious, high-reward employee suggestion programmes.

At the very outset of Benchmark, one of the characteristics of BAe that I thought justified a culture change programme was the incredible mix of good and bad practices across the company. In some activities we were real star players, in others we were losers. If we could collate the former attributes, we'd be at the high end of EFQM scores. It was therefore in our best interests to deploy the EFQM standard as a magnet to draw out the really top-flight practices that we could then seed and distribute across the rest of the company. The issue was how to activate latent ability, as well as to identify and quickly remedy areas of weakness.

Innovation and technology issues

BAe boasts considerable technological leadership and high-quality products. Yet we doubted that we had moved forward fast enough in the generation, capture and exploitation of new technological opportunities. The Innovation and Technology Value Team also found that there was insufficient economic discipline around the innovation function. There were just too many stories where techies had taken the law into their own hands and spent time and resources to arrive at answers to problems that were scientifically interesting, perhaps, but did not have real-world application. And there were too many stories of different business units working on overlapping problems and not sharing data or insights. The NIH disease (Not Invented Here) was widespread. The Value Team identified many instances where the company seemed incapable of delivering technology at the right place, the right time and the right price.

This was particularly distressing since innovation and technology are a core competitive arena. We had to stop squandering the advantages we possessed and improve our competitive differentials, by generating innovation, then quickly transferring it among business units, then applying it swiftly to market opportunities. The impact of roughly half a billion pounds of annual research outlays had to be greater if BAe was to forge an unassailable leadership position.

We see dramatic proof of our technological prowess every time a new aircraft takes off from the runway. But ideally we'd like to see innovation in both a broader and a more pervasive sense: innovation should infuse more of what we do, not just our elegant end product. We aspire to be innovators in the entire gamut of business functions, from how we create and present proposals to customers to how we approach planning, to our personnel and compensation polices. This entails risk. It depends on a culture that is comfortable with radical departures from tradition, that is willing to overcome historical inertia and re-examine any particular policy or process, deconstruct it and build a newer, better model from the ground up. Via Benchmark's culture change we had a chance to attack the many-layered encrustations of tradition, and a culture where all too often an innovative idea was put down with 'we don't do that around here' or some other form of conceited dismissal.

Benchmark is a moving target. Today's benchmark will be below the median tomorrow. The only way to keep pace is with an appetite for new ideas and an ability to create genuine innovation. The Innovation and Technology Value Team looked outside BAe to gather data and get a good fix on other corporations' methods, achievements and benchmarking practices. The team studied many companies, including Hewlett-Packard, 3M, Brother, Sony, Rank Xerox and Kawasaki Heavy Industries. They looked for ways to:

↑ develop meaningful targets for innovation;

↑ create an innovation-friendly and economically responsible environment;

↑ engage the workforce in continuous innovation.

Many people think that innovation and technology are strictly about technical invention. There are, however, many non-technical or quasi-technical areas where innovation can flourish and realise business benefits. The innovation that occurs at BAe draws on only a little technological novelty. Small changes, tiny nuances, things seen from a slightly different angle, these are key to success in this area. Changing processes and methods can reflect a great deal of innovation.

Here are some of the recommendations advanced by the Innovation and Technology Value Team:

↑ Create systems that support technology development and technological transfer.

↑ Build a technology plan, corporate wide and divisional, to set high-reach, breakaway targets of achievement.

↑ Incorporate individual merit in innovation into compensation formulae.

↑ Set up a BAe technology board and spur cross-divisional technology sharing.

↑ Create a company-wide Chairman's Innovation Award to dramatise the need for innovation in all aspects of company operations and reward top innovators.

Partnership issues

Few big British enterprises depend as much on partnerships as does BAe. Partnering touches every activity in which BAe engages, both internally and externally. Only through the medium of many partnerships can the company generate the breadth and scale to go up against its larger US rivals. With a total of 28 major international partnerships, involving 250 different linked projects, one might conclude that this was an area of excellence. Alas, that was not the case. Although there are several instances of good partnering at BAe – both with outside manufacturers and internally across business units – there was no coherent and widespread understanding of the factors that contribute to partnering success. And there were also partner relations that were fraught with problems and frustrations. Each time we started up with a new partner it was from scratch. Most of the accumulated knowledge in the company was not deployed in the new situation.

Our shortfall in the partnering dimension was a drain on resources and a clear inhibitor of profits. The lack of fertile partnerships with suppliers affected costs and quality as well as timely and appropriate deliveries from them. The opportunity costs in this area were astounding. Before the BAe–Marconi merger, aggregate BAe purchases from 3000 different suppliers of goods and services were equal to three-quarters of total end product sales. In other words, BAe directly controls 30 per cent of the stuff that goes into turnover. However hard we work that 30 per cent, the greatest opportunity lay in enriching the supply chain partnerships. If we could build relationships that would give us first crack at suppliers' best ideas, if we had good communication about mutual opportunities and problems, the eventual bottom-line impacts could be significant. Potential of the same order of magnitude existed within BAe, where interdivisional transactions run just short of a billion pounds a year.

So the Partnership Value Team scrutinised our partnerships with other manufacturers, with suppliers, governments, communities and intra-BAe. The team's overall mission was to come to grips with some really thorny issues, like understanding ways that organisational cultures influence inter-partner conduct, or questioning what it would take to get business units to share good and bad partnership experiences with one another. Accordingly, the Partnership Value Team advocated the following behaviours to enhance partnership skills:

↑ Foster a climate of trust, respect and understanding between partners.

↑ Seek joint approaches to problem resolution and the pursuit of opportunity.

↑ Maximise the vitality and openness of knowledge exchange between partners.

↑ Adopt mutual measurement and improvement goals with partners.

↑ Understand the way culture and behaviour influence how partners think and act.

↑ Encourage business units to share experiences of partnership success.

People issues

That our people were alienated and disengaged was substantiated by opinion polls showing employees' lack of confidence in the leadership and their non-belief in a happy and prosperous future with BAe. In 1994 we polled the employees of the biggest divisions. We were dismayed when we compared our results with average results for UK corporations as a whole. Key questions covered were:

↑ Understanding how the company expects to achieve its goals.

↑ Worker confidence in leadership.

↑ The quality of two-way communication.

↑ Career opportunity and job satisfaction.

↑ Understanding customer needs.

↑ Delivering to customer requirements.

↑ Devotion to quality.

In nearly all these indicators of morale and efficiency, there was a huge and worrisome gap between ourselves and the basic norms in the external UK commercial environment. An internal survey of young people at BAe demonstrated that their expectations in such key areas as training, future career prospects and job security were nowhere near matched by realities. Little wonder that in a survey of opinions of graduating youngsters by the *Sunday Times*, BAe ranked 34th, a miserable score for a company of our national stature.

Our record with people was particularly embarrassing. And while so many UK companies had striven hard to be global competitors by finding new and fruitful relations with employees at all levels, we certainly were not among them. That was a finding of a survey we conducted of our major defence subsidiaries, Military Aircraft Division (MAD), Royal Ordnance (RO), Systems & Services Division (SSD) and Dynamics (D). In each of these key areas, we were well below average – usually by at least 20 points.

Here are the results of responses to eight key issues, compared to a national benchmark measure.

Issue	Best BAe Unit	UK Average
Our people understand how the company will achieve our goals	46%	65%
We have confidence in our leaders	24%	40%
Good two-way communication exists	28%	45%
Career opportunity satisfaction	20%	55%
Company's future secure	42%	55%
We understand customer needs	58%	89%
We deliver to customer requirements	50%	63%
We rarely allow other considerations to override quality	27%	42%

It is hard to convey the frustration I felt when I looked at this negative data. From where I sat I simply could not believe that they reflected the truth. My experiences indicated that the company was full of bright and motivated people at all levels. And the survey data did indeed substantiate an upbeat view in a few areas: BAe employees, for instance, did rate the company pretty highly in feelings of loyalty and pride. And the really heartening good news

– which dovetailed nicely with Benchmark's entire philosophy – was the fact that many workers felt underemployed and wanted to do more within their jobs.

Still, we were nowhere near benchmark in the people department. The People Value Team would have to do a lot of heavy lifting in the coming years. The cure they advocated was sweeping and radical. The behaviours they urged for boosting employee motivation and involvement included:

- ↑ Create a heightened sense of job security.
- ↑ Build systems and methods for new skill and knowledge building.
- ↑ Keep hand on pulse with regular, issue-driven opinion surveys.
- ↑ Managers should be all-round role models and the bearer of all five values.
- ↑ Encourage risk taking and permit failure.
- ↑ Criticise ideas and conduct, not personalities.
- ↑ Make teamworking the dominant lifestyle.
- ↑ Use peer or 360° reviews and job appraisals.
- ↑ Establish personal development metrics.

Process solutions to the people value were far easier to come up with than new behaviours. Indeed, the people value contained within it some dangers, in so far as it opened senior management to the possible charge of insincerity. Because if you say 'people are our greatest strength' and subordinates reply 'No mate, you don't treat us as if those little words have meaning', then the two perspectives have to be resolved. The danger is that employees will misinterpret the intent of the people value and imagine that it is more democratic than is in fact the case. So they then say: 'Why don't you listen to our ideas? Why don't you engage us in the things that we think are important, rather than keep hammering away at what you say is important?'

One of the causes of the disappointing survey results was the low level of expectations entertained by senior management about the typical employee. 'The workforce was expected to hang up their brains with their jackets in the morning,' says one personnel manager. 'They had never been given any sense of involvement in anything that was going on. There was no challenge. The very early stages of the transformation programme were really illuminating: through very simple things, like total quality training programmes, we discovered that people really did want to make a contribution, and they really did want to change the way things were done, and they really had some damn good ideas about how things could be improved and (by the way guys) how you could manage with a lot fewer management and supervisor types.'

In Benchmark, we in a sense wanted to have our cake and eat it: to keep the BAe traditional command-and-control structure, but simultaneously to open up the company to a more participative, team-oriented management style. And the conduit for this, of course, was role modelling by BAe leaders. As Benchmark gathered steam, our managers showed that they were increasingly open to suggestions and input and deeply committed to meeting others' expectations of decent and transparent conduct and, what's more, willing to take criticism. But – after all the teaming and debating and brainstorming – the leader would be the one to make a decision on which way to proceed. Nevertheless, everyone who had participated and given of their creativity and brainpower would feel that their individual voice had been respectfully heard. That was the ideal that glittered on the Benchmark horizon.

I think that Tom Nicholson has said it better than I can: 'There are some 4000 leaders within Military Aircraft and Aerostructures. Not all of them will want to make the journey to the new culture and not all of them will find it easy. It is difficult to manage a group where on the one hand you say to the members: "You as individuals can make a contribution to this discussion. But at the end of the day, when we're talked out, one of us has to make the decision on which way we go." The difficulty (culturally for us at BAe) is getting each of those group members to feel that their individual voice was heard in this discussion – even where their views did not prevail. So they've got to feel engaged, regardless of the outcome. And I don't mean management textbook stuff: the problem is turning it into something real where, for instance, it would be perfectly acceptable where the individual says: "Well, I really don't like the decision that has been arrived at here. I am fearful of the future consequences. But at least I had my say in it; I was given the opportunity to participate and at least I do understand why that decision was taken." That would be real.'

That completes my sketch of the five Value Teams' first pass at their areas, their analysis and diagnosis. Each Value Team had to sell its approach and recommendations to the entire 130 Group, a critical audience if ever I saw one. A couple of times the 130 Group demanded that a Value Team go back to the drawing board and come up with something better. By forcing each Value Team to earn approval of its approach and recommendations, we ensured that the ultimate users would be more likely to support these value statements and adopt their concomitant behaviours.

At this stage in our progress, I was pretty confident that we were on track. We had a good vision statement that supported our strategic plan, and values and behaviours that were in the hearts and souls of the top management cadre, and we'd also defined those behaviours that correlated with the values. While the Value Teams had been at work, the 130 Group had continued to meet quarterly and there were signs that among them Benchmark had gained respect. 'In the beginning I thought vision and values were for the birds – the sort of stuff that helps sell management books. Besides, I wasn't a particularly people-oriented person at all,' says Mike Willis. 'Yet the level of my thinking has changed dramatically. I've learnt a lot and it has made me a more useful person to the business already.'

A culture change project is not a hothouse. Perceptions about Benchmark were influenced and coloured by what was happening in the business environment. Fortunately, rising revenues and profits supplied some emotional gasoline, raising the *esprit de corps*, although Benchmark's chief impacts to the bottom line were still some years in the future. Throughout 1995 BAe shares had one of the best run-ups in the FT-SE 100, rising by almost a third – thanks to a fatter order book in defence; staunching the operating losses at regional aircraft; strong cash generation; and market share inroads by Airbus into Boeing's dominance in civil aviation, to name but a few factors. 'The management of BAe is in good odour at present,' said a study that synthesised the views of a dozen institutional investors. 'It is particularly encouraging, given past history, to report that BAe is increasingly seen as having a balanced team at the top with an appropriate combination of skills.'

In a little over two years, BAe had gone from being an object of derision in the City to a company of which great things were expected. While some self-congratulation was called for (after all, in a shrinking overall market, the BAe order book was up more than a third in two years), we had to guard against euphoria and a *laissez faire* approach to culture change. So I frequently reminded our people that we remained a recovery stock and that by some important measures we were hardly in a position to beat our chests. A £100 investment in BAe the day I took over as CEO would be worth £153 at the end of 1995, while £100 in the FT-SE index would have climbed considerably higher, to £187.

There was therefore still work to do, and Benchmark was the tool for doing it. In the next chapter, Colin describes the many contradictory forces unleashed when an organisation sets out consciously to change its values. His comments set the stage for Chapter 6, in which I narrate our first efforts at translating our new values into actions and practices.

Dear Dick

I found the workshop a useful experience in terms of networking across the corporation but found it patchy in terms of benefit from the material presented. I expected to hear a bit more about just who our partners are and what our strategy/tactics towards these partners is.

***

Dear Dick

I found the day both motivating and disturbing. Motivating because people were interested in what I had to say and hungry to discuss it further afterwards in the bar. Disturbing because I saw at first hand the cynicism about the '130 Group' (the very term itself is clearly divisive) and possibly even more worrying, a large population that were totally unconvinced of a need to change. 'It isn't broke, so why are you trying to fix it ?', that came across loud and clear.

***

Dear Dick

I was, however, very disappointed in the lack of leadership that was shown by the Value Team champions, one of whom did not even stand up and show his commitment to the Value. I do think the process is now 'tired' and does need a change in direction.

***

Dear Dick

It came across very clearly that there are no common practices with regard to customers within BAe: this needs to be addressed urgently.

***

Dear Dick

I think the syndicate work at this workshop was rather mechanistic, process and model oriented. The danger of this is that the Benchmark aims may degenerate into something akin to political correctness, rather than based on personal and corporate conviction.

***

Dear Dick

It is absolutely critical to understand who the customer is and who makes the decisions. The Ministry of Defence is not monolithic. Some very real decisions get formed at quite 'junior' levels. Understanding the customer top to bottom is absolutely important and also making sure he is not confused by too many British Aerospace people selling him the same thing.

***

Dear Dick

During the feedback session the Military Aircraft and Aerostructures top management were the most inanimate group of executives I have ever seen. Yet I know them all personally – some very well – and the majority can be most animated. I do not feel the workshop helped one iota in moving their opinion. We can go through the motions, but unless we have proactive leadership, it will be a bland overlay which absorbs resource without specific benefit.

***

Dear Dick

Analysis: A) Inadequate coverage of how we manage 'unreasonable' demands of our customer. How do we shape expectations and win competitions whilst only making deliverable commitments when competing against less scrupulous competitors. B) A need to recognize different natures of customers and individuals within the customer organization. Different behaviours will therefore be needed to delight them.

***

Dear Dick

The ongoing debate as regards internal customer versus external customer is to me a sterile argument. I do not believe that you can have a different set of values or behaviours between internal customers as to those which you reflect when dealing with external customers. People should not consciously have to change because of the 'status' of the customer with whom they are dealing. Most of the short term opportunities for adding to British Aerospace's value will be fulfilled through improving our internal customer relationships against the corporate vision of making British Aerospace No 1. It is my experience that 'demanding customers make for good suppliers'.

***

Dear Dick

I would also observe that the presentations probably told us more about the ability of senior British Aerospace managers to make competent presentations based on limited substance rather than the quality of the underlying work.

***

Dear Dick

We are a company which has always relied heavily on individual customer contact and connections. I have no problem with this and think that it is highly effective at the front end, and we can all cite specific individual achievements. However, behind all this is teamwork, and passing on the benefit of our experience. We as individuals continue to be protective and secretive in this area.

Dear Dick

As a company we are product focused and not customer focused and whilst the attitude of 'we are Warton and we know best' or 'trust me, I'm from Warton' is diminishing, there is still some way to go.

***

Dear Dick

I thought much of the work presented was anecdotal and simplistic, and there is much more work needed.

***

Dear Dick

In order to help the syndicate process, I would like to suggest that a significant part of each future workshop has an educational theme, perhaps in lecture format, when we can learn from external specialists more about some of the tools and techniques used to date, and others which we might deploy in the syndicate sessions.

5
HIGH-INTEGRITY IMPLEMENTATION

'Frustration is part of the terrain of change. In fact, while the literature often portrays an organization's quest for change like a brisk march along a well-marked path, those in the middle of change are more likely to describe their journey as a laborious crawl towards an elusive, flickering goal, with many wrong turns and missed opportunities along the way.' So observe Rosabeth Moss Kanter, Barry A. Stein and Todd D. Jick in *The Challenge of Organizational Change*.

That is the truth. Change management is often portrayed as an idealised process, conducted by heroes, visionaries, charismatic leaders who like Moses take the children out of Egypt. That is mythologising what is a very drawn-out and arduous business. Changing corporate culture is like hacking a path through the undergrowth of a jungle with a rather blunt machete. Each corporate jungle is unique. However, everyone encounters similar obstacles on their way.

This chapter studies one of the key challenges that the hacker will confront: translating aspirational values into concrete meanings and actions. To this point the 130 Group had been basically wordsmithing in their meetings. Now they had to give the values direction and substance.

To my mind there are four broad phases of any radical change programme:

1 The diagnostic phase.
2 Setting goals and envisioning those ideals towards which the programme must move the company's people and organisation.
3 Achieving transition states and milestones along the road.
4 Evaluating the results.

At this point in the story, Dick Evans and his top folks were hacking around somewhere between phases two and three.

All the phases of culture change programmes are interdependent: each has to be executed well. One cannot get on the starting block with values that are trite; one cannot interpret good values in a clichéd way. Note the rigour with which BAe management undertook each phase, how they proclaimed really good foundational ideas and then fleshed them out with interventions that claimed hearts and minds. Note, too, their use of the top executive cadre for conceptualising, directing and finally executing huge chunks of the transformation. The drawback, in terms of duration, was more than offset by the solidity and integrity of the programme.

To help the reader understand the quality of BAe's achievement, the how, what, when and where that Dick described in the last chapter, I will now compare their actions to some other corporations struggling to effect culture change.

Let's start with value setting. What, in any case, is a value? The question has perplexed thousands of managers who have been through culture change programmes. When all is said and done, there is a fuzziness on the edges of the word values. But this much is clear: a value is something alive in an employee – a thought, or a feeling, that is habitual and recurring and that determines his or her conduct.

Good or bad, spontaneous or self-conscious, values are widespread and they run deep. They inform people's intelligence, effectiveness, social cohesion; or determine the lack of these factors.

Values affect the worker's perception of work as purposeful and effective; or the contrary, as wasteful and aimless. Values foster mutual trust or mistrust. They spur or frustrate motivation on the job. Values stand outside an organisation's authority structure, coexisting with it. They induce group cohesion and the right conduct and prioritise an individual's decision making. Values can be subterranean or out in the open, cryptic or easily defined. And they can spur a company to greatness or doom it to oblivion.

Change management programmes alter culture by looking at an organisation's operant values and by deciding which of them should be modified, and which new and good values should be considered for adoption in the light of the competitive environment. 'Good' is based on one criterion only: relevance and adaptation to the competitive environment. Creating this framework is the responsibility of top management. Through reflection and debate – often protracted, ambiguous, circular and frustrating – they will arrive at a cluster of aspirational values that they feel are closely linked to the factors of competitive success.

Allied Signal's Larry Bossidy, whom I mentioned in my last chapter, has lately put the $13 billion US industrial giant through major restructuring and cultural change. He observes that in the beginning: 'We had to unite ourselves with vision and values. And that effort began with the team at the top. We had an off-site meeting of the 12 top managers. We spent two days arguing – and I mean arguing – about values. That was helpful, because at the end of the meeting, we not only had the values, we also had a specific definition of each one of those values.'

The degree of sincerity and commitment in these internal debates determines the quality of the resulting value statements. It is precisely here – on the grounds of sincerity and authenticity – that the Benchmark programme is notable. Throughout the entire project a significant number of the top management group strove for, in the words of George Rose, now the company's Finance Director, 'high integrity implementation'. And because they succeeded, the values they cultivated have proved to be powerful agents of transformation.

The task of translating aspirational values into business practice has four steps, each progressively more difficult than the last:

1 Aligning values to strategy.
2 Actively communicating values.
3 Shifting values through organisational actions.
4 Business leaders role model values in their behaviours.

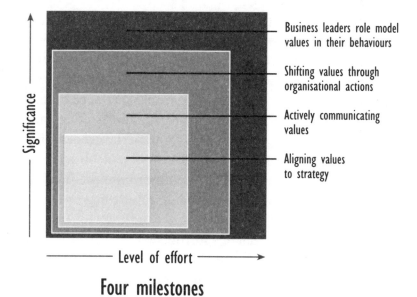

Business leaders role model values in their behaviours

Shifting values through organisational actions

Actively communicating values

Aligning values to strategy

Significance

Level of effort ⟶

Four milestones

Change management efforts are kicked off in the inner left-hand box and progress outwards. At each phase the programme generates greater impact and significance, and demands greater effort and resources.

Aligning values to strategy

It cannot be said often enough: economic success depends on a corporate culture that fits hand in glove with the strategy. Corporate culture is a decisive competitive weapon in a great number of industries, particularly service industries and sophisticated manufactured goods. To deliver shareholder value, management has to be ruthlessly objective with judgements about the degree of fit between their culture and the hard-edged facts about their competitive arena. Often managers think that there is a benefit to espousing a 'feel-good' culture, which is more a reflection of their personal values, or wishes, than it is an attempt to guide employee behaviour for strategic and competitive ends. It is perfectly legitimate to have a culture of truth, love and honesty – provided that those are the values that work best in the marketplace, not otherwise.

It is equally legitimate to develop a culture of aggression, meritocracy and internal competition – providing that this is what a particular market dictates. 3M fosters a culture of strong internal competition between divisions, in part because it wants to spur new product innovation and has found from experience that inter-business unit rivalry achieves that. Similarly, there is a dog-eat-dog culture in the trading departments of most investment banks, where meeting the numbers is the only criterion of job survival. To make such a place less aggressive would not fulfil the investment bank's goal of profit maximisation. Moral: culture must be directed and governed by strategic intent.

At BAe the strategic challenge surrounded and permeated every Benchmark event. At all meetings of the 130 Group, Dick Evans spelled out in detail the reasons for competition intensifying: the latest mergers of the US behemoths, the inexorable logic of European defence company rationalisation, the entry of new producers from previously less developed countries, like Israel or Brazil. Once this point was driven home, he beat the drum for culture change.

All successful culture change depends first on the articulation of a strategy, second on determining which cultural values support this strategy and which undermine it. What is more, the articulation of those values has to be exact, succinct, readily communicable to all employees. The values must have a meaning that everyone can express in action.

No big corporation has a unitary culture. Different geographic locations, different departments, different levels in the hierarchy, different functional disciplines create their own subcultures.

Striving for a uniform culture across the whole of a large organisation is neither possible nor desirable. What management should look for are half a dozen or so values that transcend all those subcultures – values that the entire organisation can subscribe to, that line up everyone's thoughts and actions with the requirements of strategy. Experience shows that there should be no more than seven, while fewer than three values is probably inadequate.

Strategy definition is usually pretty simple. Most strategies are quite easy to get down on paper; as was ours to focus the entire business on defence and aerospace. By contrast, value work is a very demanding exercise. It requires much debate and interaction. Executives easily get bogged down in ambiguity, in semantics, etymologies and buzzwords. Discussion leaders and facilitators are constantly challenged to keep the fires of enthusiasm burning. This process takes time. And it takes deep thought, because the strategy/culture connections are not always obvious.

The most common mistake made by managers in value-setting sessions is to strive for originality. They want to make their company's expression of values sound different from those of peers and competitors. However, there is no payout from this approach. Values must be inclusive, inspiring and motivating. Inevitably, they will be very general. There will also be some overlap between values. Cynical minds may seize on this to declare: 'Oh, but we've heard this stuff so often it must be tosh.' This doesn't matter.

In the final analysis, the competitive advantage of values lies not in their articulation but in their implementation, their manifestation in the workplace. And in this activity corporations differ, often dramatically. According to a *Fortune* magazine article published in October 1998, there is a huge difference between the corporate culture and conduct of high-performing companies and those of the run of the mill. Like many, high performers profess to value teamwork, and customer focus, and fair treatment of employees, and initiative and innovation. The difference is that they pursue these values relentlessly. By contrast, merely average companies focus on minimising risk, respecting the chain of command, supporting the boss and making budget. Other values clearly take second place. The *Fortune* article confirms the thesis that values have massive economic outcomes.

Allied Signal's final line-up of values was a very basic seven: customers, integrity, people, teamwork, speed, innovation and performance. 'They're not unique,' Bossidy observes. 'But they're important because they give all our people a view of what behaviour is expected of them. And if you're a leader in this company, you risk being labeled a hypocrite if you don't behave according to those values. And you're going to get some heat – and that's terrific.'

At SmithKline Beecham the values that Bob Bauman and his team finally arrived at contained strong echoes of those that BAe would affirm some five years later. They were as follows:

Performance
The company must be performance driven. We continuously aim to improve performance in all we do.

Customers
We aim to be customer oriented. We strive to provide products and services of superior value to meet expectations of our internal and external customers.

Innovation
We will constantly strive to be creative and innovative in all endeavours. All employees are encouraged to bring forth new and better ideas for improved performance, whatever their responsibilities.

People
Our employees are all partners, working together in the pursuit of the company's mission and strategy. We strongly value teamwork, and we want every employee to be motivated and to succeed.

Integrity
We demand openness and honesty throughout our operations to engender trust, and integrity underscores everything that we do.

We believe that every activity must be able to pass the test of public and internal scrutiny at all times.

It isn't accidental that these three companies have separately come up with rather similar value sets. The differences come in the implementation. I think there is a good litmus test for a value: does it immediately suggest specific ideas for its realisation? Merely saying that people are important does not pass the test: the issue is how or what aspect of people we are talking about and how this connects to competitive competence. Each company will answer this question in its own unique way. Values will not result in corporate transformation unless they are discussed in terms of the particular behaviours that support them. If managers cannot explain to someone who works for them what living the values means, the whole programme grinds to a halt right there.

At BAe, the first line of value-enacting behaviours were quite general. They included:

- encouraging BAe people to realise their full potential;
- to work against targets to be the best and continually measuring, challenging and improving the way we do things;
- striving to be our customers' preferred supplier, our suppliers' preferred customer, as well as a respected partner in our industrial alliances.

The second-line behaviours were more specific. These included:

- Setting specific performance measures and improvement targets for each customer that are validated by regular assessment of customer perceptions of BAe performance
- Open and honest two-way communication with customers and partners and within BAe – expressed in the slogan that came into common usage, 'to say what we mean and to do what we say'
- Engaging every employee in setting and reviewing challenging and measurable personal goals and providing others with opportunities for personal enrichment and growth.

Such definitions align behaviours and actions with the values and, in turn, to the strategic mission of the company. And here we arrive at a second opportunity for failure. If the connection between values and conduct is weak, this weakness will eventually undermine the project. Without those links, values remain simply empty altruism, impotent to effect change. Parenthetically, values are not eternal truths set in stone. They are values for now, for today, they tie in with the present strategic picture. Changes in the environment may trigger the need for new values, or a reinterpretation and redirection of existing values.

BAe was unstinting in its value work. It always examined a prospective value in the magnifying mirror of reality. For instance, there were some pretty intense discussions about elevating 'integrity' into a BAe value, and likewise 'leadership'. But while 'integrity' in dealing with issues (internally and externally) was a worthy aspiration, it was not in the end elevated to a value status – in part, I believe, to achieve simplicity and clarity in the five-value package that did get adopted.

Actively communicating values

By communication I mean something more than the common expression of thoughts and impressions in language. In a culture change programme, the only communication that counts is communication that connects – with people at all levels of the organisation. It must have the simplicity of a good advert, but also other dimensions. Parables, stories, examples and legends do the heavy lifting here. (One of the often-told legends of Benchmark and the comeback of BAe is about Dick Evans' visit to Scotland following the £1 billion write-off in 1992, when he was humiliated by investors, but took it with customary unflappability.)

The primary communicators have to be the chief executive and his top team. Communication can't be delegated to public relations or human resource departments, because they lack the organisational authority and moral clout to be change champions. It is a mistake to think that communication is merely formal announcements, releases, programme brochures, posters and so forth. These are necessary to be sure, but they are also superficial and easily mocked by cynical staffers. Real communication depends on managers who have internalised the values and communicate them in everything they do – in tone of voice and style of interaction. Leadership and communication are inseparable. And communication will not be effective unless it is heartfelt; and this applies from the chairman to the foreman on the shopfloor.

I don't favour dramatic full-scale 'launches' of change programmes, though they are quite common. I think that they run a risk of threatening top management's credibility. The proof of communication is in its effect, not in a fanfare. Highly dramatic launches create expectations in people that will not be met for a long time, thus they are likely to engender scepticism.

In essence, big-blast and large-scale communications run the danger of creating a 'rain dance' effect, where everyone dances for joy, but when the rain stops it is business as usual. For the same reasons, I do not advocate the use of such symbols as T-shirts, coffee mugs, posters etc. This symbolism suggests that change is easy, that it is here already, or just around the corner. Nothing can be gained from underestimating the difficulties.

BAe in fact made no formal announcement of a corporate change programme. There was no starter's gun: 'Bang! The change programme is launched.' Rather it proceeded incrementally, a slow unveiling in which more of it was gradually revealed to the entire workforce through Dick Evans' public addresses to employees emphasing the simple goal of wanting to be the best in the industry. Subsequently, he incorporated the five values into this company-wide message. In time, the full Benchmark was delivered through more videos, company publications, training and educational instruments; meanwhile the top managers in the various business units spread the word, person to person. Thus a groundswell built and achieved scale.

BAe was an organisation that needed change desperately, yet in many ways opposed it. The level of unhappiness and frustration over dysfunctionality was very high, at times and in places almost neurotic. In this condition the company was far from alone. An operant culture may be deeply negative and Kafkaesque, and yet still most people will resist a change initiative and blindly defend the status quo. The BAe culture was 'strong', in the sense that it had a high opinion of its talents, particularly with regard to technological accomplishment. It was incapable of admitting the damage that its arrogance and easy forgiveness of its faults wrought on its relationships with the customer population. BAe was a real 'I'm alright Jack' kind of organisation. Benchmark had to combat and undermine this 'strong' culture at its roots, which entailed determined and unremitting communication and role modelling of the five values. Dick Evans was nothing if not relentless. Over a period of four years, he sat through every minute of every Benchmark policy and strategy meeting and workshop. Without such unequivocal signals from the chief executive, I doubt that Benchmark would have achieved its success.

Corporate life is loaded with signs and symbols. Chief executives radiate them in what they do, and what they choose not to do. Dick was an extraordinary chief in his unconscious capacity to command attention, because he is venerated as the man who brought the company out of the desert, because without the revenues from his big Saudi Al Yamamah contract the company would have gone down the tubes. Dick is a natural-born salesman, with as many close relationships outside BAe as inside it. He is at home hobnobbing with heads of states, chiefs of the big US defence megaliths, and chatting up the procurement heads of customer nations. He is also physically a restless, high-energy fellow. By sitting through entire days of serpentine debates and discussions, he allayed many participants' anxieties and suspicions. The fact that he didn't leave the workshops to take outside calls, didn't even (as many did) talk on his mobile phone during breaks, generated a widespread trust in the process.

Shifting values through organisational actions

A common problem in change programmes is that they degrade into mere exhortation and encouragement. Rhetorical and propagandistic gestures about the need for change are rarely effective, and will in most cases provoke criticism and resistance from employees. What's more, culture change has to be undertaken with a good grasp of the limits and impotence of the customary exercise of power. In a culture change situation, management achieves its goal tacitly, through suggestions not orders, signposts not commands.

The *Fortune* magazine survey found a clear correlation between the real culture and the espoused culture in high-performance companies. This relationship is key. In a project like Benchmark, it takes a great many initiatives to improve the fit between the real and the ideal culture. But the really big guns of change making are not 'soft' but 'hard' factors, like a focus on productivity, performance and profit. Many corporate change programmes place too much reliance on people stuff, probably because they are so often planned and dominated by the human relations staff.

Now let's look at each of the forces that actually can be deployed to create value shifts. First, there are the basic ingredients of culture that influence values. Second, there are value-related factors, such as philosophy and symbols, which affect value formulation. Third, out of values there come the actual behaviours that advance, or fail to advance, culture change. Fourth, the peformance gains emerge.

Let's take up these topics in sequence and go deeper into how an organisation can change values.

Leadership actions reinforce or undermine the goals of the change programme. Leaders of high rank rarely perceive how very visible their conduct is to the people several levels of authority lower down or their capacity to provoke anxiety, disorientation and/or alienation. Caught up in a change programme, people often become starved for information that will help them read the terrain and foresee the future. They become mesmerised by the chief executive and his immediate circle, eager for any clue that their minds can fasten on. They imagine if they look closely enough at how the bosses get in and out of their cars, walk in lobbies, say good morning to receptionists, do or do not blow up at some little screw-up, they will get a bearing on what's happening.

Like the emperor and his new clothes, many top managers act as if the change programme is just another thing the company is doing, oblivious to the fact that they have, willy-nilly, altered the climate of the corporation and changed the light in which all things are viewed. Employees cannot help thinking that leaders are the personification of the organisation, that their every action expresses the organisation's beliefs, values and assumptions. Say, for instance, that a chief executive drives to work himself in a saloon car and across the street there is another chief executive who has a chauffeured Bentley. The first communicates values that identify with the workforce, while the second expresses the thrill of being a top dog. Neither value is better than the other. Each has different ramifications for the culture. When a change management programme is launched, all the leaders' deeds and actions on the job will be interpreted in the light of that programme's goals.

At Intel, the great semiconductor maker, there has been a deliberate effort to eschew all signs and symbols of executive rank, as a way of emphasising the all-pervasive truth that Intel is a technology company in which everybody's input counts. So there are no reserved parking spaces, no executive lunch rooms, no corner offices (the CEO has a cubicle no bigger than the average programmer's). Intel employees are immensely proud of this egalitarian meritocracy. Many visitors to the company are shown the CEO's cubicle, because it is a cultural icon.

Performance measures are in many ways the DNA of a culture, the genetic factor that makes working in one company so different from another. Cultures vary in what they measure and how they measure. Some will emphasise individual contributions, others will subsume individuals in groups, teams, collectives. Measures affect how managers think and act in terms of risk, the pursuit of innovation, ability to think long term etc. Before Dick Evans launched

Benchmark, the performance measures in use were a perfect expression of a culture that regarded financial measures as a second-order effect of its engineering, design and manufacturing skills. A great deal of financial measurement went on at BAe, mountains of stuff, so people would be prepared for any question that might crop up. (The kind of data that guarantees that nobody can trip you up!) But since nobody focused on the interpretation or analysis of this data, it was, for the most part, useless as a tool for running the business for maximum profit.

Each of the BAe baronial business units had different accounting methods and different rules for computing operating profits. The accounting people at headquarters then had to restate divisional numbers for purposes of consolidation – whereupon they became gobbledygook to the divisions. Result: these measures not only failed to guide decisions, they conveyed the message that lax accounting was tolerated in BAe. Benchmark created the conditions in which myopic accounting disappeared. But it also ended up using the annual cash-planning cycle in an entirely new way that has achieved a huge improvement in resource allocations and profit yield.

People practices are clearly the basic clay of a culture. This is reflected in how people are selected for employment and promotion. Some companies look for a type, favouring, for example, independent entreprenurial people over those who are looking for a lifetime employer. Others want heterogeneity. In some supervision is heavy, in others it is light. Some motivate with sticks, others with carrots. Some spur internal competition, others suppress it. BAe's people practices emphasised specialisation and compartmentalisation. Not only was there a stockade around each business unit in terms of transfers of people, but within divisions there was little interdisciplinary movement. Individuals who'd made big contributions to a particular defence contract were hoarded like gold, far too valuable to be shared with other parts of the business. The result was a strong *esprit de corps* in contract teams. Unfortunately, none of it spilled over into the larger company.

Vision, *purpose* and *strategy* influence the culture, just as the culture reflects back into these three elements. If an organisation's vision and strategies are muddled, its culture will become a muddle as well. A culture sets the limits of a possible strategy. If, for instance, a company follows a strategy of market share dominance, it will need a culture that recognises the business benefit of such a strategy. Likewise, failed strategies have cultural impacts. In the case of BAe, the business units assembled by Margaret Thatcher's privatisation gurus 10 years earlier were a pot-pourri. When Dick Evans took charge, they were all possessed by a kind of organisational narcissism. It was only after major asset disposals and the attainment of its present strategic focus that BAe was in a position to consider altering values, so as to inform and strengthen the strategy.

Structure affects values in the way power and information are (or are not) channelled and shared. Structure is largely a matter of tradeoffs: control vs spontaneity, rigidity vs improvisation, scale and complexity vs simplicity and the beauty of the small. Structure is rooted in an organisation's competitive circumstances and corporate history and thus varies from industry to industry and, often, from geographic region to geographic region. Dick Evans faced a structural 'disconnect' at BAe. For legal and shareholder reporting purposes, BAe was one company with one balance sheet, one group of supporting banks. But this was only on paper. In fact, the corporate centre had little influence on the business decisions made at the division level.

Dick learnt this the hard way. In the 1992–94 period the post of pan-BAe corporate marketing director and a support organisation were created. The man given this job, Jerry Wooding, remembers the tensions it unleashed. 'The managing directors of the business units immediately said: "We can't entrust the business winning authority to a guy at the centre who is corporate, a man who doesn't feel the real heat and burden of the division. So we're not going to trust him."' Wooding ended up as a fall guy and Dick took flak from both sides. 'Give me the responsibility and I don't mind taking on the challenge,' says Wooding. But the business units refused. 'I got blamed for everything: either I didn't win a piece of business or I did win it, but they complained that the price, the conditions, the margins just weren't good enough.' Wooding's attempts to create an organisation that linked to the business units 'got rubbished … chewed up by the managing directors of the business units,' he says.

This and similar experiences taught Dick that shuffling the boxes of the organisation around, or band-aid solutions like appointing corporate tsars of this and that function, would be to no avail. As for forcing the business units to meld and combine, that was anathema, given the degree of hostility between them. Bereft of organisational fixes, there was no other option but to chase culture change.

Competitive context concerns a number of things:

⬆ the youth or maturity of an industry in its lifecycle prospects;
⬆ numbers of competitors;
⬆ market share distribution;
⬆ determinants of success;
⬆ government regulation – to name but a few.

To state the obvious, the culture of a big mining company will not be like that of an Internet start-up. BAe's competitive context was in flux, principally because of the end of the Cold War. The expected industry turnover, the numbers of competitors, the quality of margins, these were all unpredictable. But one thing was predictable: BAe lacked the kind of culture that could cope with much exogenous change. Out in the business units in about 20 sites dotted around the UK, there were thousands of managers suffering from that old British disease: sentimentality about past glory. They belonged to the legacies of Hawker Siddeley, De Havilland, Avro, British Aircraft, which in times past had all competed against one another. To them BAe was merely a shell, lacking a vivid identity.

Another critical aspect of BAe's competitive context was the company's tendency to see the market in very parochial terms – as a great British asset entitled to special protection by the Ministry of Defence. Dick Evans sought to change that outlook and educate everyone in the company about the daunting fact that the real competitive context was the entire globe. If BAe continued to compare itself only to UK players, then complacency and smugness would be the result. By restating the competitive context as international, and comparing BAe to giants like McDonnell Douglas and Boeing, the truth was brought home to all managers: they would have to change or suffer grievously in the rough and tumble of this marketplace.

Business leaders role model values in their behaviours

This is unquestionably the most significant factor of success in change management efforts. It is also the one most commonly overlooked, and thus the most frequent source of the many failures on record. The first three phases – aligning values to strategy, actively communicating values, shifting values through organisational actions – proceed perfectly, and then, wham, the change programme falls on its face because the importance of leader role modelling is underappreciated. The blame is cast at the feet of the technique or tools of change management. But change management is not about tools, or processes, or rules. It is about how people – all the people – in a corporation behave. If leaders do not 'walk the talk', no one else will either. Subordinates quickly see through all signs of non-conformity: they immediately detect lack of commitment by the leadership to the highest standard of execution.

Earlier I described how employees scout about for clues to the lie of the land. Now I point to the likelihood that they will misinterpret the behaviour of seniors, never giving it the benefit of the doubt. Even jokey, off-hand comments by a leader about the programme will typically be seen as a betrayal of its value. I recognise that such 'winking' or mild sarcasm or drollery is often nothing more than a harmless way of letting off steam. I don't blame people in these programmes for wanting to poke friendly fun at the heavy tone of the workshops and training programmes, the almost churchy atmosphere. I often give in to the temptation myself. But mild derision and humour about a change project should be resisted. And this goes for all workers, not just the leadership. Newborn culture change programmes create insecurity and a binary mindset: are you for or against it? In reality, of course, each thinking individual will buy in to some aspects and have reservations about some others. But colleagues and co-workers won't usually take the ambiguity into account: they want a simple check-off, yes or no. And humour at the expense of the programme indicates 'no'.

As with everything in corporate life, there is an authority structure within a change programme. There are initiators of change, who perceive the need and who understand the strategic imperatives. And lower down there are recipients of the change message. Thus all change management programmes proceed from the ranks of senior executives outwards to the larger population who had no part in their early formulation.

As the programme moves down the organisation and away from the centre, it is subject to dilution. Values that look very attractive in the boardroom may sound like stupid platitudes elsewhere in the organisation. Those engaged in value work should remember this, and find simple and truthful expressions that resonate with the rank and file. As one US academic has wittily observed, 'Visionary light, like any other, diminishes in proportion to the square of the distance, so it may not shine very brightly out on the shipping dock or in the union hall down the street.'

One of the ways that the light can have strong wattage is through the vividness of the leadership behaviours that reflect the values. A case in point: Derek Wanless, Chief Executive of NatWest Bank, has publicly announced the kinds of personal behaviours that he will strive to excel with. He has vowed to spend less time at meetings, to get out of the office one day a week to see customers or get into operating situations, and established an executive director's hotline that anyone can call with a question or comment.

Benchmark has been such a success because of its unswerving focus on leaders' role modelling of values. The members of the

130 Group, by changing their own behaviour, went a long way to destroy the old culture of interdivisional rivalry and arrogant aggression and disdain of other units. They learnt to listen to others, to seek feedback, to explore the chemistry of human interactions. They also expressed a commitment to quality in things big and small; for instance, the 130 Group workshops were always held at first-rate facilities, the invited speakers were top drawer, the facilitators and consultants in many fields among the best in the country.

They also were tough minded in appraisals of whether or not they were living the values. It is easy for very senior managers to deceive themselves on this. A good reality check is to study a diary. Top executive diaries should reflect the values promulgated by the change process. If they don't, this has to be corrected. Some years ago I worked with the chief executive of a large energy company that had undertaken a sweeping change initiative. This man claimed to spend most of his time on human relations issues. But when I checked his calendar, I found he spent less than 10 per cent on people! He promptly changed his behaviour to fall in line with his espoused values.

Clearly, this man believed that change management programmes can be delegated. They can't. To delegate the core responsibility to others is to sow the seed of failure. Such failures are rarely publicised. Nobody is at the end of the race saying 'hey – we failed'. The change project just peters out and dies off at some early phase. We estimate that of those companies which have attempted change management, around 50 per cent have done good work on aligning values with strategy. Only 30 per cent have completed the second phase and successfully communicated the values to employees. BAe is one of the few contenders that have really penetrated into phases three and four, achieved any kind of shift in values, while its leadership has made an exemplary effort at supporting and realising the values in thought and deed.

One final point about all four key phases of change management that we've studied in this chapter. Behind each there always has to be momentum – a hum, a quick and eager pacing, a shared sense of going towards new territory. Every programme starts with buzz and excitement. But the enthusiasm will not endure on its own. It has to be stimulated and supported. Discouragement can so readily develop over something as intangible as culture change, whose unfolding always seems far too slow. Momentum is the antidote to entropy. In the next chapter, Dick describes how BAe kept the spirit alive as it slowly disseminated the new values throughout the organisation.

6

NOW FOR THE NUTS AND BOLTS – THE BENCHMARK ACTIONS

Our marathon discussions of values had bright and shining moments, and moments that seemed pretty sluggish. One minute the discourse reflected great clarity and the group achieved strong common understandings, but the next moment would be muddled, when it was difficult to know where the verbiage might be leading. Others in these brainstorming sessions also experienced these surges of forward motion and regression, of hope for change and frustration – whereupon many started calculating how much time these events were stealing from the mounting pile of work, and the crises, back at the office. Yet there was no other process whereby we could stitch together the truth about ourselves and the BAe culture. This was a talking cure. It was the only way out of our limitations and our history.

I should make an important qualification, in case the reader gets the wrong idea about BAe. Benchmark initiated a company-wide investigation and discussion of shortcomings. This was both difficult and, as we have seen, necessary. Because this narrative focuses unflinchingly on BAe's dark side, some readers might imagine that everything was rotten in the woodpile, that the company was a lumbering giant, slow witted and behind the times. That, of course, was far from the case. Before Benchmark, BAe did a lot of things right, some things brilliantly, and not only in technical areas but in matters like high-end software and complex project management. The issue the 130 Group addressed was how BAe could become more brilliant and thereby ensure our future competitive success against the rising combat levels in the marketplace.

To accomplish this we had to take a good, clear look at ourselves, our strengths, our weaknesses. This self-analysis is the prerequisite to cultural transformation. To do this analysis rigorously, pulling no punches, requires an organisation that already has a fair amount of self-confidence: enough so that it can confront faults and blemishes, whose acknowledgement will be the springboard of change. I'd warn other companies against the temptation to do the analysis quickly and shallowly; it will backfire.

Our values nailed down, I thought it important to get quickly to the next stage, to move from the abstract to the concrete and figure out those actions that would best reflect and support the values. So the members of the Value Teams did their research, consulted with experts and made site visits to benchmark installations. In total we ended up with several scores of actions, which had to be pared down to a manageable number for practical reasons and to avoid 'initiative overload', a frequent complaint in programmes of this sort. 'A relatively small number of initiatives can have a wide effect – if they're the right initiatives, and if you pursue them vigorously. Once you get some successes under your belt, some movement, some early "wins", the process begins to generate a momentum of its own,' explains Roger Hawksworth, Director and Chief of Staff, who served on the People Value Team.

The men and women on the Value Teams had learnt much about how and why present behaviours and actions at BAe had come into being. Now they had to switch gears. The time for excavating and explaining the past had ended. The time had come for creating the processes, programmes and behaviours that would allow the company to move into the future. To do this, we all had to break with familiar patterns of thinking and conduct. This is easier said than done. Notwithstanding our failings as an organisation, it bristled with a great deal of pride (overly much so, in my opinion). I wanted that pride preserved, yet better justified with good practices and attitudes and policies.

Each of the dozen actions I describe in this chapter were created to catalyse one of the five values. An action accomplishes this act of realisation in one of two ways. Either it removes some practice or feature of the landscape that previously blocked or inhibited the realisation of a value – thus releasing potential – or it moves the company on to new ground, thereby creating breakthroughs that advance a value and take us closer to being benchmark. I describe each of these actions at some length because, as I said earlier, it is only in the implementation that the idealism of the values gets projected into real-life situations.

Some of the actions clearly have more impact than others in realising a value. Some are sexier than others and some more easy to implement. Not too surprisingly, given the pivotal role of the people value, some of the highest-impact actions, in terms of effect or recognition by the workforce, stemmed from our desire to be a model employer, at least equalling, if not exceeding, the very best practices in the UK. The result was a series of actions that announced the beginning of a new epoch in our labour policies and convinced many that other big changes were afoot.

Says personnel chief Terry Morgan, 'You don't want a programme that is perceived as having a delivery date that is far off in the future. Therefore you have to deliberately create some "hits", some early wins that get people motivated for some of the longer-term and more difficult stuff to implement. Something that people can point to in moments when they are feeling a certain amount of battle fatigue.' And the fact that we did speedily achieve benchmark status with the people-based actions was an instantaneous and lasting morale builder.

Action to support the performance value:
Value Planning

Many change management programmes try to run primarily on communicating messages. At BAe we have not done that. Instead, we have tried to push the five values down through the organisation, so that they are seen as operational needs and requirements. Although the Value Plan is one among over a dozen actions, it is the real workhorse of Benchmark. We are constantly striving to help people to create better Value Plans with more stretch and detail.

The company historically worked with an annual business planning cycle. Alas, that plan was more ritual than substance. Combined one- and five-year plans were done by the head of each business unit, who then sent the plan to headquarters, where it was filed and forgotten. Next year the same thing happened. The previous plan would be dusted off, then revised and sent to the corporate centre where it was very rarely consulted. As a tool for running the business it was a little feeble. The Performance Value Team decided that this had to stop and that the entire planning process should be given much greater relevance and impact throughout the businesses and at all levels. The Value Plan sets goals for:

⬆ the business units;
⬆ the teams within them;
⬆ the individuals within the teams.

It is something of a hybrid, in that it contains the traditional finance-based ingredients found in the conventional business plan, plus goals and targets that define how the five values are to be advanced. This sweepingly new type of plan was at first considered very radical.

The corporate plan had historically been a confidential document and many worried that widespread dissemination of plans would reveal important competitive material. We have found it easy to delete any contents of the plan that would reveal secrets, without in the least diminishing its usefulness as a rallying point for Benchmark behaviours.

Value Planning synthesises hard-edged business data with Benchmark values and with the progress we've obtained in realising the values. Performance against the values can be measured on a scorecard designed for this purpose. Thus the elements of the overarching corporate plan are cascaded downwards and outwards from the centre to progressively smaller organisational entities, ending up with the smallest team. But it is basically the opposite of a top-down plan. The Value Plan is assembled on a modular design, so that business units and then subunits, then teams within those units, all have their own Value Plans and hence clear targets against which to manage. Consequently, everyone understands the ingredients of the total plan and their own contribution to its total effect.

The actual machinery that accomplishes this is called the Team Based Value Planning process. And it is supported by a workbook, which presents a number of useful tools and techniques and processes to help teams and individuals make good plans. An upper manager at one business unit says, 'I think that some of the businesses at first thought that Value Plans were souped-up business plans, that they'd be able to simply take the conventional plan from last year and update it and add a section on BAe values, and hey presto. Soon they began to realise how a Value Plan makes you think about the business in a new light. I found it a more taxing exercise than I expected – and far more rewarding, too, in terms of understanding the business and getting the commitment from people around the core issues.'

There were, I must admit, some drawbacks to this approach: the usual issues that come up when one adopts a very participative procedure. The execution of the Value Plan depends on many thousands in the company understanding its underlying logic and its processes. This takes a great deal of educational effort. And inevitably there will be some people who require a lot of hand-holding. In fact, I have had focus group type meetings with some younger employees who have complained, variously, that it is 'verbose', that 'the message is lost', that it 'needs to be focused'. And we've listened to these very sincere objections and tried simplifying and improving the way the Value Plan is projected and explained in the organisation. Whatever its demerits, it is still one hell of a lot more credible than the distant, top-down and fundamentally powerless planning that it replaces, because it engages thousands of individuals in plan creation and plan fulfilment, and confronts them with the challenge of living the values as they do so.

Action: Business Excellence Review

This is the methodology we are using across the company to implement the EFQM (European Foundation for Quality Management) self-assessment model. Needless to say, a performance model of this type is crucial to hitting our Benchmark targets. It enables us to see a total corporate picture of performance, which can be used to drive best practice sharing.

Here's how it works. Each business unit creates a portfolio of evidence that captures its chief operating characteristics, according to definitions in the EFQM model. Subsequently, trained EFQM assessors – there about 200 of them in the company today – go to work on scoring the portfolio's key ingredients and track back to the workplace those key issues that have been identified. Then the assessor team (the majority coming from outside the business unit) sit down and have a feedback meeting with the business unit management team about the key strengths and weaknesses, whereupon an improvement plan is developed. These improvement plans and goals get incorporated into the business unit's Value Plan, so that the challenge is totally clear to everyone. When the assessors find areas of good practice, these are captured, documented and shared across the corporation.

After the first round of this process, business units' best scores were compared to EFQM winners. The results showed that we had some real evidence of first-class practices within many of the units, but not all of them. The data also showed widespread weaknesses. The advantage of the EFQM approach was that it imposed an external perspective on what is authentically benchmark, and defined the size of the gap that would have to be closed by BAe.

Action: Value Based Management

Creating value is the goal of all economic activity. Thanks to recent innovations in management knowhow, there is a powerful new tool that allows companies to forge stronger links between their internal operating measures and the dynamics of shareholder value creation. Conceptually, Value Based Management (VBM) is a system designed to make employees think and act from a shareholder perspective. In essence, it reveals how almost every possible action and decision has an impact on cash, either now or in the future.

This approach is not fundamentally new. Discounted cash flow models have long been an important analytic tool for making new investment decisions. VBM extends the discounted cash flow methodology to existing operations and reveals which are creating and which are destroying value – information that is not directly available from conventional budgeting and accounting. In the past, BAe produced significant quantities of accounting data of many different kinds; while this material was of some use in running the business, traditional accounting does not really depict the dynamics of value creation and has the additional drawback of focusing too much on the short term.

VBM works through performance indicators that have direct links to cash generation. Under VBM, business units get analysed for their appropriate value drivers (these differ from industry to industry) that expose problems and opportunities. Often they match, or overlay, Benchmark activities. For example, in a business where it can be demonstrated that customer satisfaction levels correlate with ultimate sales, there might be a clear link with the Customer Value Team. Once we are tracking the right performance measures consistently, our decision making improves dramatically. Needless to say, VBM results correlate with other performance actions. EFQM, for example, dovetails with and complements VBM. The customer value also correlates, since dissatisfied customers will have a negative impact on long-term cash generation.

Aside from the sophistication of measures, VBM has another important characteristic: managers are given incentives – their bonuses are tied to shareholder value creation. Because VBM is capable of recognising the degree of risk in an investment, and gives proper weight to time-adjusted cash flows, it has given BAe a laser-like focus on how we generate shareholder worth.

A VBM pilot programme at the Royal Ordnance Small Arms Ammunition unit showed that a relatively small improvement in half a dozen 'value drivers' would lead to dramatic improvements in rates of return. It also showed that this business unit had some customers that were not adding to value creation. According to the VBM analysis, many of Royal Ordnance's export sales were not value creating. They only looked profitable by conventional accounting measures, which simply compared price to cost of production. However, the VBM analysis revealed that the complexity of export sales generated costs that were buried in other functions of the business. These costs were literally invisible using traditional accounting methods. VBM dispelled the illusion that this was good business practice and immediate remedies were put into place.

BAe was not an early adopter of VBM. But we have made up for that in the strength of our commitment to using it as the means to realise the performance value. VBM is a great tool for clarifying the really important management agendas and for distributing a common, pan-BAe language and perspective. It is a strategic tool for top management insights about future scenarios and how they might unfold and affect cash generation. It is also a wonderfully clear instrument for capital appraisals, for make-or-buy decisions and for budgeting working capital.

Actions to support the innovation and technology value: Chairman's Awards for Innovation

One of the Benchmark goals was to spur a dramatic surge in the number of ideas generated by employees. This could only be done through the democratisation of innovation – i.e. if the entire work-force believed themselves capable of significant contributions in this area. Hence we launched the Chairman's Award for Innovation, a talent search followed by a grand show to acknowledge and reward those who had shown creativity and innovation. This has become an important annual celebration of idea generation (scientific and non-scientific equally), both at the business unit and the corporate-wide level. In 1998 there were over 700 nominations and many hundreds of awards. The highly publicised prize gives emphasis to the one-company concept and sends the message for the first time in BAe history that brilliance at innovation is much sought after.

Here are some highlights from the last three years of Chairman's Awards, in which the number of nominations from around the business has more than doubled:

- A team from the Chatterton site recognised the need for a highly accurate panel loading system. This would provide the benefit of allowing one of the machines to be run without interruption. The result: a doubling of output, and because of the higher volumes that were possible a new customer was won.
- At the Airbus Design & Derivative Products Group, employees came up with a reorganisation of project management that led to bottom-line savings of £8 million.
- Royal Ordnance, maker of ammunition used by the UK police, recognised that this customer needed, but did not have, sufficient training in use of small arms. To obtain a competitive edge, Royal Ordnance agreed to undertake a shared partnership with the development and operation of shooting ranges.
- A joint BAe team from three sites worked on just-in-time inventorying of carbon fibre composite material, currently used

in the Airbus and soon to be used in the Eurofighter. The result: significant reductions in inventory holding costs. Previously this material arrived once a month in 100 metre rolls. These were tested, then stowed in refrigerators. Four to eight weeks passed between receipt and use of the materials. Thanks to good forecasting techniques and intelligent supplier interface, twice-weekly deliveries now arrive thawed at point of use, in smaller quantities. There are also huge economies in packaging materials.

⬆ A supervisor who attended a continuous improvement workshop was surprised and dismayed to find that his operation was part of the course material: it was the worst case, an example of what not to do. The particular operation coats 300,000 or so components annually with corrosion-resistant cadmium at our Samlesbury facility. The supervisor was determined to remove this stigma and he and his team put in improvements that greatly increased output. Two years ago they cadmium dipped about 4000 items per week. After the changes, the rate was 15,000 and there were fewer rejects.

⬆ An Airbus factory manager had long been vexed by the problem of rivet wastage on the production line, due to the fact that rivets of different sizes are lumped together in bins. Some also fall out of the bins. The cost of this waste was £600 a week for Airbus, or £30,000 a year. One day strolling through a supermarket this factory manager had a Eureka moment: the standard tubs used to dispense nuts and raisins might make perfect rivet dispensers. He was right, and consequently waste cost declined.

⬆ A rescue training team at Chadderton sought to create a training package for putting out fuselage fires, which are very difficult to suppress and must be handled in a very particular fashion. The team hoped that their training package might be sold to internal and external customers, such as flight crews and aircraft customers. There was one obstacle, however. To meet regulatory requirements, the team had to replicate the conditions of a real fuselage fire. They found an abandoned fuselage that was destined for scrap and, using their own time and tools, they refurbished it for £600. The facility has been a success. Many hundreds of people have gone through their course, which has also become a source of external revenues for the company.

Action: the Innovation Forum

In any large company, all senior managers work flat out on the daily tasks of administration, liaison, meetings, supervision, crisis management, planning budgets etc. One of the last things they are likely to have time for is to sit back and meditate on looming technical and socioeconomic trends that will affect the business in the future. The BAe Innovation Forum is a senior management vehicle for visioning salient trends and likely impacts on products, processes and competitive positions. This annual two-day meeting explores technology and innovation in BAe and lays the groundwork for new knowledge building. The programme calls for presentations by outside business leaders, futurists, academics and boffins.

At the Forum, senior management considers the possible business impact of numerous geopolitical and technological scenarios and paradigm shifts. The goal is to 'think the unthinkable' and look for 'the enemy in the sun', a fighter pilot metaphor for what is unseen and indistinct in the future and yet could be swiftly upon us. During the programme, people from our Sowerby Research Centre report on existing and proposed R&D projects. At the conclusion of this tour of the big picture, Forum participants have a much firmer grasp of those aspects of technology and innovation critical to the future bottom line. Armed with these insights, we can discuss them with customers to assess their revenue potentials.

The Forum is designed as a mind-expanding experience, to foster the breadth and intellectual vision that are so vital in an age of technological convergence like ours. More concretely, it offers a field for role modelling for leaders, since here we see them focusing very deliberately on the issues that will affect the technology of products several generations into the future.

Action: intranet

These days no self-respecting technology-based company dares to neglect the tremendous potential of intranets as a means of better communication and interconnectivity. They are a tool for information and best-practice sharing of an altogether new power and intensity. In part because of heavy profit and cash constraints in the mid-1990s, BAe was not in the forefront of UK corporations exploring these technologies. But once our recovery had some vigour, we investigated their potential. As a first step, in early 1997 we installed 2000 Web browsers. A year and a half later there were more than 15,000. Total investment to date is £5 million. At least four-fifths of top management are consistent intranet users. Web pages support both corporate and business unit knowledge sharing, including much of the statistical data that tracks many facets of Benchmark progress.

Although this is a great tool to fulfil Benchmark goals of creating a seamless coherence and interaction between the business units, in truth we have proceeded cautiously. Clearly, one day we will have a global intranet that is 100 per cent secure with the kind of intense connectivity that now we can only dream about. But we will get there in small steps, not a giant leap. It is typical of the BAe character that we are determined to analyse the cost justification before paying out a lot more money on an intranet. We don't want to build something very powerful only to find it vastly under-utilised. At BAe we are inclined to be sceptical of the capacity of information technology to change behaviour. We prefer to foster a behaviour, get it entrenched, then put in IT systems to facilitate it.

Actions to advance the people value: the involvement process

Values don't just float in the sky like white puffy clouds on a summer's day: they have to be brought down to the everyday level. What is more, people must be involved in realising the values at all levels. Hence it was important to ensure that everyone signed on to Benchmark and helped realise the one-company focus. A useful tool for both generating and measuring such effects is the employee opinion survey.

Surveys had been done in the past at the business unit level. In November 1997 we did the first corporate-wide survey at all UK and overseas installations. The response rate was very encouraging, 58 per cent. To me this indicated that BAe employees had a lot to say and sought greater involvement. That we were going to the trouble of soliciting their views indicated that corporately we wanted a greater connection to workers everywhere. The areas investigated in this landmark survey were leadership, supervision, long-term goals, dedication to quality etc. The data thus gathered formed a baseline for periodic 'dip-check' surveys, with which we have continued to measure progress, or lack of it, as perceived by employees.

In the past the business units had conducted employee suggestions schemes. These varied from location to location – some of them were fertile, others were not. Here was a perfect instance of how we could use Benchmark to generate an improvement across the entire enterprise. In 1996, our Aerostructures site designed and piloted a new suggestion scheme. This has since been disseminated to other business units. It has stimulated individuals and teams to challenge the status quo and to arrive at creative alternatives. Employees whose suggestions are adopted are awarded points on the basis of the usefulness of their ideas. Points entitle the employee to make purchases from a special catalogue. The participation levels vary between business units. On average they are about 50 per cent (compared to an old participation rate of around 20 per cent) and contribute significant bottom-line benefits – £4 million in 1998, we estimate. As Mike Rouse, Group Managing Director – Military Aircraft and Support Systems, observes: 'Benchmark has created a climate in which workers are happy to put forward ideas, knowing they will be sensibly reviewed and, if they have merit, implemented.'

Action: Personal Development Plans (PDPs)

One of the things that disturbed me most about our employee survey results was the high proportion of young people who felt they didn't have a bright future with BAe. This would clearly erode the foundations of the enterprise, if it continued for many more years. If you say 'people are our source of strength' and 'people are our future', how do you manifest that conviction? One way might be to have clearly established lines of advancement, education and training. But those we had were haphazard and most individual employees were pretty passive about looking at development issues and seeking ways to advance through the organisation. Result: skills and professional abilities often stagnated.

In one of its boldest proposals, the People Value Team said that every one of our 46,000 employees should have a Personal Development Plan (PDP) that would adhere to a common format across the company. These PDPs would be kept up to date and would be used in discussions with supervisors and members of natural work teams, for career planning and skills enhancement. Thanks to this formal system for self-appraisal, there would be open discussion of goals, career targets, training needs and behaviours that contribute to satisfaction and accomplishment. What is more, PDPs are integrated into team Value Plans, which in turn are expected to address the development needs of individuals.

PDPs encourage employees to discuss their personal development goals with their team leaders and to create a plan, with a timetable, for achieving these goals. They also facilitate the creation of different behaviours that may lead to more fulfilling work experiences for employees and at the same time focus their activities on the goals of the corporation, i.e. boost what is sometimes called 'economic literacy'.

When I say that all employees must have a PDP, I do mean all. I have one, so do all the executive directors. And although we are a little long in the tooth, we too can get something out of sitting down and reflecting on our areas of strength and weakness, and considering what kinds of knowledge, or experiences, would help us handle the job better. PDPs, incidentally, are not boilerplate. They can be as simple or as detailed as the individual wishes. But all are signed and dated by the individual and his or her team leader or manager, so that they act as an informal contract. And they are not one-off or even annual exercises, but roll on continuously.

Action: Benchmark Employer

Several interrelated actions move us towards our goal of being an organisation where there is broad equality in working conditions and benefits and perks and where differences in individual ability are reflected only in the pay package. For us this marked a major break with past practices in UK industry. The Benchmark Employer concept has harmonised reward and recognition across the company.

We used to have a private health scheme for managers, for example. Says Terry Morgan: 'But in the Value Team we questioned that and asked "If we are a Benchmark company, why do we think our managers are more important in health terms than non-managers?" So the old restricted scheme was replaced by one open to everyone.' It was the same with car leasing. In addition, the People Value Team urged the adoption of a 'security of employment' agreement that assured all workers that in the event of redundancies in one business unit, every effort would be made to find alternative positions elsewhere in BAe.

Let me give you some specifics on the health care scheme and the employee car scheme.

Health care
In July 1997 the company launched an elective supplementary health insurance programme, called Excel. With 6000 members enrolled, it ranks as the largest single corporate health scheme in the UK. Excel offers self-funded, comprehensive, private medical care at more competitive rates than most other packages on the market. It is not an insurance plan, like PPP or BUPA, but a

collective, non-profit corporate fund into which all members pay the same rate, regardless of age, location or grade. Contributions are determined by cash inflows and claim outflows from the fund. The greater the number of participants, the less each individual needs to pay. Factors like a history of smoking and pre-existing conditions are not taken into account. Initial members could join unconditionally, that is without a medical exam or questionnaire, and there is also the option of a paid second opinion.

Employee car scheme

Although car-leasing schemes for managers are pretty entrenched in the UK, employee surveys show that those who are not entitled to this perk feel some resentment. In the light of Benchmark's people value, leased cars had to be democratised. You can't say to some apprentice machinist, 'We value you a great deal but unfortunately we can't give you the same car options as your boss.' So the old rank-based car-leasing programme was scrapped and any employee with more than one year of service may lease Rover cars at very attractive rates. The programme was initiated in June 1997 and some 3000 people had signed up at the end of 1998 – a rate of enrolment far in excess of estimates.

Action: profit sharing

A workforce with an economic stake in the business is bound to give more of its enthusiasm and talents than one that has no ownership. Many surveys have shown that employees want to share in the success of their enterprises. We have responded to this need with a democratic profit-sharing scheme that is designed to inspire a sense of commitment and greater involvement in everyone, regardless of rank and pay. When the company exceeds its profit targets, all employees receive an equal allotment of free shares. The exact number is announced at the end of each financial year. These shares are tax free after the three-year retention period, earn dividends throughout, and entitle the holder to any bonus shares that may be given out and to vote like any other shareholder. After three years they can be withdrawn, transferred to another person or sold.

The scheme is funded from a percentage of operating profit increases over certain targets and in early 1998, based on 1997 results, the first grant of shares went out. It got the attention and excitement of the people on the factory floor, for many of whom this was the first time they had owned any share investment. But importantly, it also sent the right kind of message: that it is everyone's responsibility at BAe to be involved in the value creation that generates share price increases.

Actions to advance the partnership value: joint venture enhancement

In defence and aerospace if you don't have partnership skills, you don't get a seat at the table. Following the end of the Cold War, partnering has become the standard *modus operandi* among the European players, since all lack a primary national government customer that can support a major aircraft programme alone. Joint venturing is inevitably going to be more prevalent in the future European and global market for defence equipment.

Since BAe has more than a fair share of the existing cross-national partnership, joint venturing is clearly a major talent at BAe. Yet the knowledge we have could be much more systematic and more easily available to others than is the case at present. This is why we have created a special group to collect partnering experiences around the company and build a database of best practices. In addition, we have been working on better tools for analysing the suitability of joint venture partners – a big step forward from the opportunistic grabbing of a partner, only to find them perhaps unsuitable later on.

Action: procurement improvement

Here was an area that we had not focused on very clearly in the past, yet it offered a rich field of opportunities. Companies that have driven hard for supply chain improvements have found gold. Early adopters of best practices in supply chain management achieved cost reductions of between 20 and 40 per cent. We set the goal of squeezing savings worth £600 million over three years from a company-wide procurement strategy covering the 50 largest suppliers.

Some 70 per cent of the products we make stem from suppliers and home contractors; over half of purchases come through just 15 suppliers. Logically, therefore, even small improvements in supplier efficiencies could have massive effects on our costs of doing business. We launched a programme to improve relationships with our 100 top suppliers, to lower acquisition costs and improve processes. Here are some of the objectives we listed:

↑ Taking customer needs and transmitting these into appropriate supplier management tactics.
↑ Better partnership relations with suppliers.
↑ Sharing best practices with suppliers.
↑ Operating a company-wide supplier development and management process.
↑ Defining and deploying the BAe partnership sourcing policy.

Action: better government relations

As I noted in the discussion of the customer value in Chapter 4, we had played a bad hand at government relations in the past. The UK government, and some others around the world, were fed up with our practices and attitudes. But for the fact that our products were first rate, we'd have been in the wastebasket of history long ago. There were exceptions here and there, but by and large our approaches were seat of the pants, depending on the business unit and the particular programme. So one of the first things we did was to decide that we had to abolish the haphazard, inconsistent and autonomous efforts of the business units and bring this activity under the BAe umbrella. Focus, coordination, structure – these were the goals from Jeddah to Canberra, Whitehall to

Washington. We improved our system of 'markers', in which senior-level defence procurement officials each have a direct counterpart in the BAe management structure. Lastly, we supported government initiatives to improve their purchasing procedures, like Smart Procurement in the UK, with workshops, meetings and colloquia.

Action: the Internal Trading Framework

Back in the bad old days, intra-BAe disputes and areas of friction and conflict between business units were transmitted all through the company. Some business units had far better relations with external than internal suppliers. This disease was in remission by the time the Partnership Value Team got down to seeing the lay of the land. But the relationship structure and the chemistries needed to be fixed. The Internal Trading Framework that the team dreamed up is designed to foster the one-BAe culture as an integral part of the transfers of goods, services and technologies between divisions. This framework calls for business units to grant all BAe entities preferred supplier status, and to evaluate internal supply matters in the light of their contribution to shareholder value gains. Somewhat along the same lines, we have improved the distribution and transfer of expertise and frequency of business unit knowledge sharing in many functional areas, like finance, community relations, public relations – this in addition to long-standing linkages in engineering fields of various kinds.

An early win from improved internal partnerships is the smoother interface between the Aerostructures unit and its internal customers. Aerostructures' relations with Airbus and the military and regional aircraft units had long been pretty strained, in large part because, for reasons going far back into history, it was not a very low-cost producer. Internal customers, constrained from purchasing wings and fuselages on the outside, complained that there were hardly any incentives for Aerostructures to be efficient, because it was effectively subsidised by captive customers. Under the banner of partnership value, both sides agreed to calculate a 'social cost' (roughly the excess of Aerostructures price over the market price) which is not incorporated into the transfer price. What is more, several of Aerostructures' internal customers have changed their purchasing and contract-letting practices to facilitate greater efficiency at Aerostructures.

Says a top manager at Avro, our regional aircraft unit that is an internal customer, 'Five years ago, we would never have come to this kind of common understanding: 1) that there was indeed a price/cost gap, 2) that it could be handled in this cooperative way. It may not sound terribly adventurous or different. Yet the fact is that five years ago all you'd have had were two bits of BAe completely at war with each other. Instead we've found an adult way that is open, understood and manageable. And it is not a battlefield any more.'

Actions to advance the customer value

Of all five values, there was no doubt in my mind that the most frankly aspirational was the customer value. In other words, it was here that the company was many miles from being a benchmark standard. However frequently we might put our hands on our hearts and tell customers 'We have changed. There is a new BAe', they had every right, given the neglect of customer issues in the past, to be highly sceptical. Some were downright disbelieving, and I don't blame them. We recognised at the outset that this was not an area where we were likely to score any quick wins until we'd come up with some highly focused actions that, over time, would erode negative customer perceptions.

Action: the customer satisfaction process model

The goal of this project was to create benchmark standards that could be applied throughout BAe (covering internal and external customers) and that teams and organisation could self-assess for:

↑ knowing the customer;
↑ understanding the customer;
↑ delighting the customer;
↑ measuring outcomes.

Knowing means knowing the people on the other side of the relationship, their roles, their influence, what they expect from BAe. Understanding means caring about their priorities and problems, and this of course entails us having a pretty good knowledge of their culture and environment – though, to be sure, that is easily said but very hard to do. The need to delight is based on the recognition that in today's environment the mere satisfaction of customer needs does not lead to competitive gains. One has to penetrate customers' consciousness with the idea that they can always count on you to go the extra mile.

Any models devised by the Customer Value Team, and any tools and techniques to support those models, would have to satisfy all the above-mentioned goals. From this there evolved a number of key actions, such as incorporating the customer value in learning and development programmes around the company and a pan-BAe reward and recognition process in which outstanding efforts in customer service are acknowledged, rewarded and shared with others.

Another action is one that I personally feel strongly about concerning 'first impressions', which have a very important bearing on customers' long-term perceptions. Everyone who works here is providing a service to somebody else; the telephonists, receptionists and drivers are a great example of this. Normally, the first person a customer talks to in our company is the telephonist, and if the caller doesn't get much satisfaction it will have an effect. When he or she visits the company, the receptionist is the first person encountered on the way in and the last person on the way out. You might have had a wonderful meeting with BAe people and solved a huge engineering problem in the process, but if you walk through the reception area and he or she tells you (in effect) to bugger off, you don't remember the success of the meeting, you remember that person's conduct and attitude.

The customer value is really pervasive and its chief manifestation is internal. We have fewer than 20 really big key customers worldwide, who happen to shop with us in mega-nought numbers. I know everyone on a first-name basis and if they have a problem they know to ring me.

The ultimate value of any of the Benchmark actions is not in their good intentions, but in whether or not they are vigorously and enthusiastically adopted by the business units. If a particular action doesn't win converts, then we might as well paper the walls with it. Fortunately, all our business units have been keen to try a more vigorous and intelligent outreach to the customer, using the actions I have described and inventing a few of their own.

Before Benchmark, the Military Aircraft and Aerostructures Division had its own serious customer problems. Now it is putting a lot of energy into convincing customers that it is worth their time and trouble to invest in a new style of interaction. 'Trying to engage our customers in this discussion has not proved easy,' observes Tom Nicholson. 'We do recognise that simply sending off questionnaires saying how we rank on a scale of one to ten is a pretty immature thing to do. Generally it does not give the customer much satisfaction, nor meaningful feedback to our people. What the customer wants is to see repeated high performance emanating from MA&A. They also want to see our ability to commit to the things that we say we are going to commit to.'

MA&A attacked this issue by reforming its internal customer systems, culture and behaviours. It made customer support a distinct activity with its own managing director. The entire internal customer infrastructure has been put under the microscope at MA&A. The division has a fix on the internal buyers and users of processes, services and hardware, and it has defined their needs and preferences. As a result, MA&A's previously functional organisation has been 90 per cent realigned around customers. Now all the organisational ingredients flow together in a stream running directly to the customer. This has created greater clarity about the customer interface, achieved by role playing the customer's needs and perspectives. We asked ourselves: 'If we were the customer, what would our demands and requirements be for BAe?' This may sound like what the Americans call a 'no-brainer', but the fact is that this looking-in-from-the-outside perspective had never been tried on a large scale.

It is early days for this initiative, but already it has generated improved responsiveness, because each contributor to customer value in MA&A is now visible and accountable, not obscured within an autonomous (and often impenetrable) functional speciality like design, software or engineering. Needless to say, a huge part of this effort has been directed at winning hearts and minds at the UK Ministry of Defence. Every unit in the company has taken a more vigorous and structured approach to government relations. Since the beginning of Benchmark, the then managing director (now CEO) John Weston had regular monthly meetings with the MOD people to iron out any issues and problems. Many other of our top people are also dealing with MOD with more energy and sensitivity than in the past. There has been a sharp drop in complaints by the Ministry of Defence about BAe's management processes. The formerly high complaint volume about specific programmes, such as the Hawk flight trainers, has also been reduced. But of course, just improving things so that complaints vanish is not our idea of Benchmark for customer service.

The dawn of a new culture

This completes my thumbnail sketches of some of the more powerful actions that were applied throughout the entire company to catalyse each of the five values. The reader who has slogged through this long portfolio of actions might wonder why there are so many. The answer lies in the fact that the values are rich and deep and many dimensioned. You can't live them with a single programme or initiative. Without high-quality actions and deliverers (the topic of my next chapter), I don't think culture change can permeate deeply into an organisation.

Note how many of the actions – like the Personal Development Plan, Value Planning and the Benchmark Employer – were vehicles to extend Benchmark to the 46,000 employees of the company. They had been told of the five values but now, with the unveiling of the actions, they could see the earnestness of our intentions and the rigorous way we intended to live up to those values. One drawback of Benchmark's design was that it has progressed quite slowly outwards from the senior core to the main body of BAe. Time and again at the 130 Group's sessions we criticised this lack of speed. But this wish had to be balanced against the need for a complete buy-in by the management group as a prerequisite to further enfranchisement.

The question of the timing and content of distributing change management initiatives is in fact very complex. You can't have the entire workforce attending the same workshops as upper management; the costs would be prohibitive. What are needed are different yet effective tools for transmitting the culture change message to the rank and file. In this regard, we have some further ideas and programmes on the drawing board that will achieve this.

I believe that many of the actions described in this chapter unequivocally signal the dawning of a new culture to all workers at BAe. A culture in which people are respected as never before, performance is measured with clarity and fairness and people are motivated in ways that satisfy both their personal needs and those of the corporation. Actions like the car-leasing scheme, the Chairman's Awards for Innovation and share ownership (to name but a few) go a long way to convey the essence of Benchmark to the 46,000.

Yet some actions become a two-edged sword. Some of them are announced, but it takes time for them to be realised because of resource constraints. This leads to a new source of frustration in the company. 'Say that someone on my staff is told that everyone is going to have a Personal Development Plan (PDP),' says Locksley Ryan, Director of Communications. '"Great," they reply. Then I tell them it's not this year but next, because there is not enough cash in the training budget. So they come back and say,

"Why can't I have it now?" Managing these expectations can be tricky.'

Everyone has found similar problems of what one might call 'cultural lag', a gap between the present and what is to come from Benchmark. Although we say that people are a key Benchmark value, we have to acknowledge that from time to time there remain indications to the contrary in the environment and in our behaviours. Like Rome, change management is not built in a day. It may require a whole new generation of BAe managers, schooled in Benchmark from their early days, for the values finally to triumph. And that could be many years off. For the moment, as Locksley Ryan observes, there is a paradox between our intent and our power to realise those intentions. Consequently, it is always easy for some critic to say, 'Aha, see, you are falling short of Benchmark behaviours.'

Benchmark has many paradoxes. For example, we were torn between the imperative that Benchmark move swiftly because of the pace of change in the competitive environment and the need to avoid cutting corners and applying a sticking plaster to culture change. Another paradox: there were continual tensions between the resources needed to make Benchmark fly and the everyday demands of the business. BAe is a heavily constrained organisation, task focused and task driven. And this was an organisation, remember, where there wasn't much management manpower excess because of the huge downsizings we had undertaken five years earlier. Another paradox and point of friction: business unit managing directors were continually being asked to deliver better and better bottom-line performance, and on the other hand we were taking more and more of their people's available time to go on workshops, seminars and training programmes.

There was another paradox, which I'm sure some readers will have picked up on. Initially, the programme had to be invested with the orb and sceptre of the chief executive, it had to be seen as an expression of my will and drive and determination. But no sooner had it been launched than it had to change tempo and be embraced by senior management as their project. And to begin with, the programme was heavily loaded with directives and instructions and signposts and definitions about culture change. But it could not remain in this condition for long. For it to succeed, BAe managers needed spontaneously to find in themselves the will and enthusiasm for change, whereupon it emphatically could not be a Dick Evans programme.

These paradoxes seemed strange in the beginning. After a few years, we got better at handling them.

Dear Dick

I continue to place a high value on the CE workshops and believe they consolidate the single company culture which is imperative across the 130 Group. I do not believe, however, that the current format of the workshops has run its course. Whilst some of the learning from the Partnerships Workshop was valuable, it was, at times, very drawn out. The syndicate groups were a good idea but they struggled through less than adequate facilitation.

***

Dear Dick

I left the workshop in the belief that it was a milestone in the change programme because your introductory remarks were forceful and timely and left no doubt regarding your commitment to the vision and your expectations of the 130 Group. I had been concerned that dissent would be tolerated and that all our efforts would be undermined by the behaviour of a few. I was glad to see we were no longer discussing whether we are going to pursue the vision, rather how – the language has changed.

***

Dear Dick

There are no processes in place across the business units for dispersing information or feedback within the company. This is particularly important with regard to experience available from operations in an export environment. For example I came across a member of Royal Ordnance in Bangkok airport and I did not even know that Royal Ordnance contracted in Thailand.

7

PARADOXES, ENABLERS AND ROLE MODELS OF CULTURE CHANGE

'Reaction to change is natural and is usually negative. This must be taken into account [when designing a change effort], explained and worked with; otherwise the change process will fail.' This quotation comes from a study by the Industrial Society a few years ago, but the thought could have been lifted from most of the hundreds of articles on culture change. That people resist change is one of these assumptions so deep that it is rarely debated.

The picture of the culture change programme battering away at the resistance of the workers is crude and inaccurate, since obviously there are forces and people in any institution that will spontaneously align themselves on the side of change. The dialectic of resistance/acceptance of change should always to be put in context: resistance about what, by whom, for what reasons. Some forms of change are welcome, they are cathartic to some, and they release potentials previously blocked. Depending on what it is, we avoid or rush towards change. If tomorrow you were offered a job in Australia at twice your present salary, don't tell me that you would not welcome the change and at least give it some serious thought.

The trick for managers building a change programme is to touch and release people's sources of personal change, with appeals to both emotion and to logic. In the last chapter, Dick went into a wide array of actions devised by the Value Teams to realise the Benchmark programme. However, on their own they would not have been sufficient, not nearly sufficient, to induce real behaviour change. To be sure, they sent out the right signals. But the signals were not enough.

In Chapter 8 Dick will describe powerful additions to Benchmark, which he calls 'deliverers', i.e. initiatives that drive culture change pervasively through the organisation. But before we get to that point, I'd like the reader to get a better grasp of this change/no change polarity and its implications for change programme strategies.

Every individual in a company has an interest in both making changes and resisting change. Certainly, we're all anxious in the face of uncertainty, a trait that goes back to our hunter-gatherer ancestors. And it is undeniable that change programmes do add to the degree of uncertainty in the environment. But anxiety is inseparable from anticipation and uncertain outcomes: fighters feel it before a fight, actors in anticipation of going on stage, footballers before a game etc. This kind of anxiety can be the prelude to triumph and to winning – this our ancestors of 50,000 years ago also knew as they stabbed a lion with their crude spears.

A 1998 study of 700 middle managers in the US and Europe by Price Waterhouse suggests that middle managers who have experienced change in recent years are happier in their work than those who haven't. More than 80 per cent of the sample had gone through three or more high-change events in recent years – usually a reorganisation or a bout of reengineering – and basically come out well from the process. These changes tended to increase the number of different job roles expected of the surviving middle manager. The diversity of their roles in the post-change environment (planning, HR coaching, communications etc.) directly correlated with satisfaction on the job. These were clearly the victors of the change processes.

The same observation is made in *Managing Change* (edited by Christopher Mabey and Bill Mayon-White), where Sue Dopson and Rosemary Stewart present a major study of the outcomes of restructuring and found that a smaller cadre of middle management jobs became 'more generalist with greater responsibilities and a wider range of tasks'. These middle managers, they write, 'had new freedoms; freedom to take on new challenges; freedom to broaden management expertise because of new responsibilities; freedom to innovate and, in some cases, risk-take.'

Clearly, then, the model of our emotional and psychological indisposition to change needs some modification! Before any change programme comes into existence, there are corporate hunter-gatherers who are likely to win, and others who will lose because their investment in the status quo, for whatever reason, is greater. If this is true, can there be natural winners from culture change, and can an individual foretell his or her chances of being a winner? As a generalisation, one can say that the team-playing skills of coordination, respect for others' views, flexibility and coaching abilities do very probably determine individual success. This is because many of today's culture change programmes, as part of their agenda, diminish or dismantle former command-and-control structures and go against the way these treat authority and communication.

Paradoxes

Of course, the likely winners don't know who they are because the corporate environment is opaque and volatile at the outset of the change programme. At every turn one encounters contradictions and unintended consequences. This makes it a particularly stressful undertaking for the traditionally trained manager who looks for clear solutions and firm rules of conduct – a dominant type at BAe. Companies on the path of radical culture change cannot readily satisfy this character type. People must embrace paradox and try to open their minds to the contradictions. To Dick Evans' list of paradoxes in the last chapter, I would add others I observed in Benchmark:

↑ *Means versus ends* For example, using 'hard' measures (cash, margins, EFQM scores) to achieve 'soft' goals of altered states of mind and behaviour.

↑ *Contradictory messages* For example, giving people plenty of time to adjust to the new values (letting speed be determined by the slowest member) then suddenly saying, 'We're out of time, you'd better get on board.'

↑ *Old versus new* For example, maintenance of old systems, protocols and practices that conflict with the spirit of the emergent culture, but have to be temporarily maintained to run the business.

The inevitability of such paradoxes readily opens up management to the charge of hypocrisy, what I call the 'you said' syndrome – as in 'you said we were going to change ... (fill in the blank) and yet really nothing significantly different has occurred.' In this way, paradox often gets used to trip up the change sponsors. The obvious reply is to say: 'You are right to bring up this contradiction. I remember that we said ... (fill in the blank) and we meant what we said, but evolutionary change cannot happen overnight. Would you (the complainant) like to offer suggestions of how we can make more progress in this area?'

In *The Age of Paradox*, Charles Handy has argued that we live in an increasingly paradoxical epoch. According to him, these paradoxes are not simply going to disappear. He warns against thinking in an either/or dialectic (either we've changed culture or we haven't, either we're a 'hard' values company or we're a 'soft' values company) and instead urges us to manage from within the paradox. His exact words: '[Managers] can, and should, reduce the starkness of some of the contradictions, minimise the inconsistencies, understand the puzzles in the paradox, but [they] cannot make them disappear, solve them completely, or escape from them.'

Underlying the paradoxes in culture change are some dark mysteries of the human psyche and genetic make-up. Culture change is paradoxical because people are paradoxical. On the surface, much of change management seems like old-fashioned common sense. Vision, values and common purpose sound self-evident, yet in reality they aren't. The language of change management, I would argue, is very deceptive in this respect – because what it appears to mean on the surface and what it actually means are quite different. Stated values are all like motherhood, transcendently platitudinous. They acquire depth, texture, meaning and power only when they are intelligently translated into action. It is only in the realm of specific actions and choices that values matter. If change-bent companies get tangled up in the slogans, the principles, the idealisations, the valorous ideals and goals, they may not put enough effort into what is key: really bringing the slogans down to earth, concretising them into process and action and behaviour and thus creating both meaning and change.

Striking the right balance

'The more unintelligent a man is,' says Schopenhauer, 'the less mysterious existence seems to him.' The same could be said of change management. The presenting reality will beguile the unintelligent manager into thinking that change management is a piece of cake. The smart one will sense the inherent mysteries and try to get below the surface. And it is at this moment, of course, that the seeds of success or failure are laid: in the exploration and attribution of meanings and behaviours. Some companies will do this phase poorly and others, like BAe, attack it with vigour and intelligence.

Looked at from a certain perspective, 'all' Dick Evans and the Benchmark programme attempted was to create a community of people that could pull together in pursuit of a common goal. But merely invoking the word 'community' when there is no community, or 'common goals' when managers are divided against one another, would have achieved nothing. Propaganda is the most frequently used and the most overrated approach to culture change. Human behaviour is not readily malleable, even when individuals wish for change and know it is in their best interest, in either personal or work situations. Think for a moment of the millions of

New Year resolutions that don't last beyond January 2! By definition, corporations cannot be any better than the people inside them. Between good intentions and good behaviour there is a vast gulf.

Inevitably, any single initiative is going to be too much for some, too little for others. And striking the right balance is a perennial problem and one that takes up a lot of debating time. Certainly, Dick Evans and his team worried about how many actions and initiatives were enough, both in terms of costs and the demands placed on people and the organisation. Many in the company wanted a relatively small package of actions, say half a dozen. My view was that they had to 'surround' the problem; that the programme of actions had to be sweeping and comprehensive. There are many faces to the resistance to change, so the change programme has to be multifaceted.

At the same time, the change project has to appear well designed and focused to appeal to employees at all levels. There is a danger that any change management project gets loaded with so many initiatives, so many good ideas for changing this and changing that, that it ends up like an overdecorated Christmas tree. 'You have to guard against a coral reef of accumulated things that have the Benchmark label,' observes Trevor Truman. In a company committed to culture change, people are highly motivated to sponsor initiatives, sometimes for the wrong reasons: 'Benchmark became a kind of seal of respectability, something that was politically correct. So we had to watch that it didn't end up like a political party, without coherence and beset with conflicting goals,' says Truman. I agree with that.

Some BAe managers tried to get the spotlight and funding for pet projects by piggybacking them on Benchmark. 'I refuse to be painted into a corner where I must make time available every time there is a Benchmark flag waved at me. My resources are limited,' comments Truman. He's right, of course. Culture change can spread over a corporation like a giant amoeba. All manner of perfectly everyday stuff for improving this or that operation can be sanctified with the icon of change management. Fortunately, BAe has many managers like Truman who know where to draw the line.

So clearly, there have to be limits and frontiers. And there has to be some rationale for the type and number of initiatives. As we have seen in previous chapters, a company needs to get several things right to make a change programme work:

⬆ a clear strategic vision backed up by values;
⬆ a set of business drivers, tough actions that affect performance and ensure the company's financial and operational health during the difficult initial phases of the change programme;
⬆ initiatives or 'deliverers' that oil the wheels of change and build commitment and enthusiasm;
⬆ changed behaviour in leaders that role model the desired behaviours.

Taking stock

At the midpoint of a change programme, it is advisable for the company to take stock, to examine its progress to date and to attempt to assess the likelihood of ongoing success. At this stage, the company's strategic vision should be clearly articulated and its business drivers should be having a beneficial effect on its performance.

It is at the halfway stage that many change management endeavours begin to fail, to display structural weakness. Many fail because they are vague, ambiguous and loaded with human relations pieties. In order to be successful, a change programme must pass a strategic test: the chief executive must be able to articulate how the organisation will gain competitive advantage in the future. 'Better products', 'better service', 'better people', such general concepts are simply not specific enough. What is needed are answers to questions like: What will be the unique characteristics of the market channels that will produce premium pricing and high customer loyalty? What will be the changes to the cost structure that ensure flexibility and low-cost performance? What brand values will be deployed to ensure that customers prefer us? The answers to these questions must be crystal clear. Employees will ask them, so will shareholders. If the top team can't articulate an appropriate response, no one will buy into the change effort.

This is not the first time I've said this, but I repeat it here because halfway through this book, immersed in all the details and tools of Benchmark, it is easy to forget the project's overall *raison d'être*. Culture change programmes can take on a powerful (and somewhat hermetic) life of their own. Participants, full of enthusiasm for the new vision, can get disconnected from the initial intent, which becomes meaningless if it is severed from corporate strategy. For instance, they go to a leadership workshop thinking that it is a 'good thing', a pleasant perk that the company is generously paying for, when the underlying truth is that the workshop has to be a weapon in the company's war with its external environment.

Along with clear and sharp vision, the top team must be able to articulate how the organisation should behave in order to capture the benefits of the new strategic direction. Simply saying 'work together, work harder, work smarter, innovate more, be more productive' is not going to cut it. How, exactly, should people do this? Behaviour is the only true currency.

Consider an imaginary encounter between the chief executive and a junior manager several layers down in the hierarchy. While it's clearly impossible for the former to tell the latter what he or she must do differently in precise detail, the chief executive must be able to give the kind of direction that the junior manager can translate into specific conduct and work practices. This is a tremendously difficult task. It is so hard to do rigorously, so easy to be trite and sloppy and superficial.

Every successful change programme should incorporate business drivers: programmes and processes that directly bring about cost or revenue improvements. Without this the culture change will be sidelined, sooner or later. To put it simply, but hopefully not simplistically, if the company's business drivers are adequate, the company's financial situation will improve, in terms of share price, cash generation and operating efficiencies. Only by incorporating the mechanics of the profit system in the programme design can a culture change programme achieve and maintain legitimacy. It is impossible to achieve culture change in a company that is not simultaneously working to improve its basic financial health. Typical business drivers might include delayering, process improvement, reducing capital expenditure, enhanced sales efforts, new product introductions.

The great thing about business drivers is that everybody can see the need for them, so they provide a rallying point. However, business drivers have a limitation. They rarely change the underlying culture of the business. Lowering cost or increasing revenue clearly brings economic advantage, but it doesn't usually address those factors that produced high cost or low revenue in the first place, because they are cultural at root.

Drivers and enablers

At this stage in a change programme, a company should be well on its way to developing initiatives that will increase the organisation's enthusiasm and commitment to change. Now is the time to penetrate and transform culture, and to alter conduct. The tools used will include leadership development, cultural surveys, vision building, team building, management development etc. In the language of management consulting, this type of initiatives are commonly called 'enablers', because that is what they do: they enable an organisation continually to change its culture. (Dick Evans calls these 'deliverers', partly to avoid using management consulting jargon and partly, I suspect, because he thinks that the term more precisely conveys the purpose of active delivery of something.)

Culture change enablers, however, have some limitations. Chief of these is vulnerability. At the initiation of a change programme everyone is thrilled with them, and the need for really powerful enablers is universally acknowledged. Everyone wants to go on training programmes, work on teambuilding etc. And everyone, too, seems prepared for the long payout that they require. However, this rah-rah mood can very quickly change if economic circumstances get more difficult, if there is a budget crisis, for example, or if there is a change in leadership. Then continued investment in enablers becomes harder to justify. Sadly, bottom line *realpolitik* steps in and the enablers get shrunk, marginalised or killed off.

In my experience, outstanding change programmes strike the right balance between business drivers and enablers. This balance is never the same from company to company, because it is entirely dependent on the circumstances of an individual business. The diagram below identifies three 'typical' positions with regard to this balance.

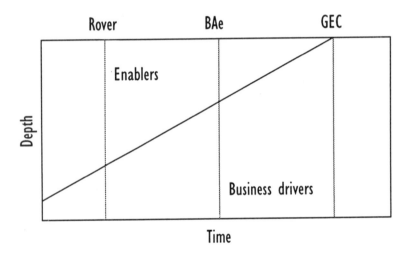

The diagram plots two variables: the depth of the culture change programme against its time horizon. Companies that are aiming for depth and traction in their change programme tend to have a strong focus on enablers. Companies that have an urgent need for change tend to focus more on business drivers. However it is possible to overdo both of these leanings. I have compared GEC (before the Marconi Electronics deal, naturally) and Rover before it was divested to BMW.

While owned by BAe, in the late 1980s Rover undertook a comprehensive change programme. This was greeted by much acclaim in the media and among academics and management gurus. It was primarily a change programme composed of world-class enablers. The changes wrought to the climate of industrial relations were stunning. The company invested awesome amounts in training and its creation of a first-class management team was impressive. However, events would prove that Rover overemphasised enablers while underemphasising business drivers. It neglected to address the underlying economic problems, such as its high cost base (due in part to ageing facilities), its relatively low market share and its excessive dependence on exports. These were all well-known issues at the time, but they were not successfully resolved. Consequently, today in times of economic turmoil Rover's profitability suffers more than most. Needless to say, these economic problems have lately been aggressively addressed by BMW. But the fact that they exist at all might lead some people to wonder at all that hype a decade ago. As a totality, Rover's change effort failed because it did not strike the right balance between drivers and enablers.

GEC is both a supplier and a major competitor to BAe. Historically, this company has been focused single-mindedly on business drivers. The financial regime was strict in the extreme. There was absolute clarity on the need to make budget. The consequence of any failure in producing margin was speedy and resolute. The managers responsible were immediately on the carpet and sometimes dismissed. This produced a business that had pretty good margins and a very tight control of cost. However, it did not build a culture of world-class performance. The amount of sharing across GEC business units was relatively low; innovation was great in some areas of technical depth but rather weak across the business as a whole; management turnover was high and morale was low. This business had relied too heavily on business drivers without sufficient investment in enablers to drive the fabric of the business towards world-class performance. This approach could not be sustained indefinitely. A new management team, headed by Lord George Simpson, previously part of the management team at BAe and who had also served at Rover, has instituted a programme to inculcate enablers that will offset the previous attention to drivers alone.

The third position on the continuum in our chart is BAe, which occupies the middle. As we saw in the wide array of actions that Dick Evans outlined in the last chapter, BAe has striven hard to get the appropriate balance of enablers and business drivers. It included a drive towards process efficiency as measured through the EFQM assessment process. It included efforts at customer retention and market penetration through the customer satisfaction processes. It incorporated the basic tenets of Value Based Management to spur shareholder wealth. One of the most striking features of the change process at BAe is the relatively high investment in enablers. Many tens of millions of pounds have been spent over a relatively short period to apply these change management techniques. There is no doubt in my mind that the success of Benchmark owes as much to the quality of the enablers as to the powerful leveraging effects of the business drivers.

However, from time to time a company should look at its portfolio of enablers and drivers and perhaps alter the mix a little by investing more resources in one or the other. That is what BAe plans to do as it goes forward, as John Weston outlines in the Epilogue. As he sees it, there is a compelling need to shift the Benchmark focus to address operational issues more forcefully.

Role models

The last in our list of requirements for a world-class change programme is that the behaviour of leaders has to genuinely change. I don't believe that it is possible to produce a set of business drivers and enablers so compelling that it will, on its own, change behaviour throughout the business. Neither of these will work unless they are accompanied by a corresponding shift in leadership behaviour. Indeed, I believe it is foolhardy to attempt to do so. If you think about the change processes in most businesses, even the most ambitious of change programmes are unlikely to affect the day-to-day work of the majority of employees in anything but a relatively peripheral manner.

If we depict the organisation in the traditional way as a triangle and represent all of the actions in a change programme as the central core, we can see the diminishing effect of them as we go down the organisation. Let's think of the BAe example. For the members of the 130 Group, the change programme was an enormous event. It consumed huge amounts of their time and affected their activities in a fundamental and direct way. I estimate that most of them were directly involved in activities specifically oriented to Benchmark for around 15 to 30 per cent of their time over the first several years of the programme. This includes attending workshops, working on the value teams, implementing the initiatives, communicating the process and so on. At their level, the embrace of Benchmark was like a bear hug. It affected the very fabric of their working lives.

However, if we go to the bottom of the organisation, where of course the vast majority of people work, the change programme was an important but less impactful process. It certainly affected every single employee directly. The employees now worked with different processes, they had different ways to input their suggestions for improvement, they received different benefits, they understood the direction of the business differently and much more clearly. But most employees were still working on the same tasks with the same equipment, with the same colleagues. So the power of the actions in Benchmark BAe to change their behaviour was relatively limited. This begs the question: how is the company to achieve the depth and sweep of change at the lower levels of the organisation?

The answer is, of course, leaders' role modelling. This is obviously only one of many things that leaders do. But Dick Evans and his Benchmark team elevated role modelling to become the vehicle of culture transmission and one that ultimately has been the key to success. The catalytic actions that were the subject of the last chapter create the space, the climate and the enthusiasm for changed behaviour in leaders throughout the business. Basically, they freed leaders at all levels to behave differently.

The accumulation of actions has a domino effect. Add one domino, then another, then another, and finally there is one that causes all the others to fall and the barriers of inertia and fear collapse. The real role of the actions in a change programme is to give the signal that it's OK to change one's behaviour. That is the real test. Some of the actions are more powerful than others; some seem to realise the value better than others. That's fine. The important question is not whether the Chairman's Award for Innovation is state of the art, nor whether the customer survey is world class, nor if employee benefits are the most advanced in the country (which they happen to be). The important question is whether, in total, the actions are sufficiently powerful to encourage people at the local level, within the thousands of micro-environments in the workplace, to look at things with fresh eyes and make those adaptive changes that improve efficiency. If this is to happen, the programme has to send out very powerful vibrations so that the factory worker will make small but important adjustments in the work process, or someone in sales will be stimulated to improve his or her behaviour with customers.

Culture change programmes in themselves change nothing. They inspire and give permission and authority to people, who in turn make the myriad small changes out of which value is created. The real role of a change programme is to provide the inspiration, the permission and the authority for leaders to make specific improvements in the business. Two words came up repeatedly in top management discussions of the programme. One was 'cascade', the other was 'embedding'. The values and the behaviours cascade down to one layer of the organisation, become embedded there, then cascade down again to the next level, become embedded and so on.

We personify a change management programme by addressing it in the third person singular. But in reality 'it' is a plural, a diverse and kaleidoscopic thing, which can be viewed from different perspectives at different times. Imagine many forces, initiatives, explorations and projects all running concurrently, sometimes interactively, sometimes not. It requires a pretty big flowchart to track all the moving parts.

It is something of a cliché to say that organisational transformation begins with personal transformation but, as Dick Evans will depict in the next chapter, this is a cliché with a lot of truth to it. Change programmes start at the top and depend for success on a management team that is willing to work hard – to change their companies and to change themselves.

8
THE POWER TRAIN DELIVERS

In my last chapter I described the catalytic actions designed to realise the five principal values and to effect a wide array of changes in individual conduct. But actions are only half the story. In addition, Benchmark needed to advance the objectives of the programme itself with initiatives that promoted change by the way they dealt with environment setting, training, communication.

These I call the deliverers of Benchmark. They are the power train of the programme. Deliverers foster a climate in which Benchmark-based conduct is more likely to occur. They broadly transmit the values, help them to seed and flourish, and change the way our minds tick.

In this chapter I am going to talk about several of the engines that drove Benchmark:

↑ leadership development;
↑ Benchmark Executive Skills Training (BEST);
↑ Team Leader Training (TLT);
↑ BAe Virtual University;
↑ the programme's infrastructure;
↑ its communications;
↑ the Strategic Leaders Programme.

Any large corporation is constantly offered packaged programmes to cope with this or that aspect of cultural change. Hundreds of consultants' yachts have been paid for with the fees earned by peddling these formulaic solutions, not all of them bad. We looked at some of these offerings, but did not bite. My preference was to inject a few highly talented individuals into the fabric of our decision making, led by my co-author Colin Price, and demand from them solutions tailored specifically to our needs. Thus the deliverers I shall now describe are mostly home grown – with consultant-specialists as back-up in a handful of technical areas.

Leadership development

Inadequate leadership had been a persistent cloud over the company, difficult though it is for me to come out and say it. The polls told us so, therefore we had to admit the problem. Poor morale usually takes many years to rectify. But given the rising fierceness of competitiveness in our markets, we didn't have the luxury of years to hone our leadership abilities.

Although there are many textbook definitions of leadership, in the context of Benchmark only one had really mattered. It is this: do the behaviours of BAe's leaders reflect the company vision and the five values? At first blush, this might not seem such a tall order. After all, the five values were common sense, not rocket science. Surely executives who boasted good educational backgrounds, successful careers and decades of experience would conform to rudimentary concepts about people, performance, innovation, customers and so on? But this turned out not to be the case. Between the intent to change behaviour and the actual doing, there was a big gap.

In May 1996, I invited Mark Hamlin, a clinical psychologist who works with organisations, to attend a 130 Group meeting. He had some intriguing ideas on leadership and behavioural psychology, which we had first been exposed to from work he did at Military Aircraft and Royal Ordnance.

Mark Hamlin stood before the group and presented a visual of a four-box matrix that located an individual's acceptance of change along a continuum of rejection, reflection and, finally, acceptance. He wanted to know where the room stood on these vectors. Group members used electronic numeric voting pads placed at their tables. A consensus response to a question can be gauged with this simple device. Individual views are melded anonymously with everyone else's.

The burning question was where the group predominantly stood, in the resisting or the change-accepting camp? The answer was not good. 'A very large number had placed themselves in the box which indicated least understanding and acceptance of the change, with the potential for the greatest level of resistance,' Mark Hamlin recalls. 'Dick was disappointed in the results, because he had thought people were well up on commitment to change.' And he adds, 'I think the reason that so many people put themselves where they did was because there remained a great deal of uncertainty about Benchmark. Some people were still not aware what it meant for them, or to their teams. They didn't feel comfortable with the process of change. Their apparent resistance to change was clearly one way in which they expressed their discomfort. They didn't believe they were getting enough information and so they didn't feel particularly supported.'

Did you catch that word – feelings? That was the tip-off to what lay ahead. After I got over blaming myself for having overestimated the acceptance of Benchmark, I asked Mark Hamlin to advise us on addressing this obstacle. At this stage I hadn't learnt an important lesson in change management: that the obstacles and blockers don't declare themselves immediately. It takes time for the resistances and lack of adaptation to manifest themselves. People hide from themselves and others, concealed behind the surfaces of executive life. One day you are in a group having a real knock-down debate on a particular issue and so you go home thinking, 'Thank God that bloody headache is behind us.' And six months later it comes back – like the Loch Ness monster poking its head up above the water – and you have to go through the same debate, only more thoroughly, hoping that this time the issue will really be laid to rest.

According to Hamlin, our remedy for the resistance to culture change was to learn something about the dynamics of human behaviour and motivation, to experiment with candour and, above all, to express our feelings, be they feelings of dismay, of wariness, or hope, of impatience with others' traits or something else. And the place to do this was a four-day workshop in behavioural skills, which he organised. In line with my unswerving principle in Benchmark matters of never asking subordinates to go through an experience that I was not willing to undergo, three executive directors and I were sequestered with Mark Hamlin for an intensive phase of self-examination and personal and group criticism.

Relating this experience subsequently to a large group of employees, I said this: 'It was a pretty humbling experience, I have to tell you, when you're locked away with a guy like Mark over many days and completely taken apart. Hamlin encouraged us to think about all the things that influence behaviour, right down to childhood factors. It helped me understand a great deal about what motivated me. I also got a deep understanding into the origin and dynamics of my colleagues' behaviour. I also learnt a lot about what makes this small team of four people work well, but perhaps more importantly, what gets in the way.' Up to then, by an unspoken agreement, we'd sidestepped some of the key issues about our conduct. We were also excessively tolerant of others' unproductive or distasteful conduct, even when it undermined Benchmark. If Joe Bloggs was dismissive of subordinates or arrogant with customers, there was a tendency in our culture to say merely, 'Oh, Joe has always been like that.' Our sessions with Mark unmasked this kind of conduct. If an organisation seeks change, it doesn't matter a damn if Joe has been a twit from the days when he wore short trousers. It is not something we just tut-tut over, we have to fix it.

The behavioural skill workshops revealed our tendency to slip into negative, off-putting ways of reacting to each other's suggestions, initiatives or criticisms. They showed, too, that we were good at indirect behaviour that masked our true feelings about a person or a situation. Feelings were not held in high esteem at

BAe. And I, as much as anyone else, was a product of that corporate background.

As Tony McCarthy concedes: 'I've been in this business for nineteen years and for seventeen of those years the behaviours which got me to the position that I am in were those which we are now criticising. Now we are saying essentially that the behaviours that served me well as I built my career at BAe are no longer acceptable.' To say this is a difficult transition is an understatement. 'Part of the problem,' McCarthy continues, 'is that people were used to seeing me as very aggressive and now I'm trying to change. So they are suspicious and asking themselves "What the hell is he up to?" and trying to see another motive behind it.'

Hamlin explained that most people go through fairly predictable emotional cycles when faced with change, whether it is a large-scale change like Benchmark or a relatively minor one. Hamlin derived his particular approach to change from the pioneering work of the American psychologist Elizabeth Kubler-Ross on bereavement. Mark explained that the 'connection between change at work and breavement is that they both involve loss – for one it is the loss of a friend or relative, for the other it may be the loss of things that have been very familiar in the work situation.'

'Of those who went through the Leadership Programme, most were very enthusiastic about the process,' says Hamlin, 'Inevitably there were some who felt less keen, but everyone left with the clear view that behaviour in the organisation had to change. In any change programme some people will always remain on the sidelines. So resistance is not surprising.'

The reason he was not surprised is that for some people the change Benchmark demanded was further than they wished to go. This is consistent with Kubler-Ross's work, which shows that some people never recover from loss. Hamlin has extended her original perceptions to identify a number of emotional stages that an individual typically goes through when confronted with change. These are:

↑ denial and disbelief;
↑ frustration and irritation;
↑ uncertainty and anxiety;
↑ depression;
↑ acceptance and exploration;
↑ commitment.

The good news is that people can be helped through the various stages. The danger in a change programme is that people get stuck in the early stages of denial and frustration. Moving people on from these phases can be hard, but it can be done through several building blocks that an organisation must put in place to achieve change. These are information, support, clear direction, involvement and encouragement.

Each of these was dealt with in the programme. It made the case for change through information and through supporting people in their expressions of feelings about change. It was crystal clear about what would be required of them in the future. And it gave lots of opportunity for participant feedback.

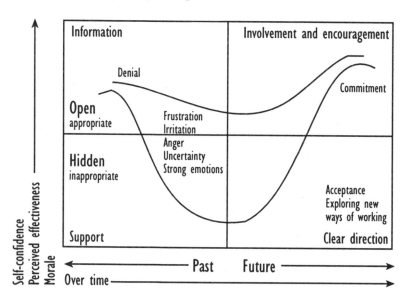

Source: Organisational resource

Experiencing this personally, together with discussions I had with Mark Hamlin about problems that he diagnosed in the organisation, I learnt that the enemy of change is often what is hidden from view, that is to say what people are not disclosing about what they are feeling. The programme provided a forum in which people were encouraged to be more revealing. In the end, it enabled the participants to move away from 'I thought I was the only one who felt this way' to the position of 'OK, we're all in this together – how can we make it better?'

There was another vital lesson we learnt from Mark Hamlin about the psychodynamics of change. An individual does not experience the different stages sequentially, leaving each one behind and over with. The process is much more complex and indeterminable, in which emotions surge up and die away, seemingly at random. Individuals who seem to have adjusted may find themselves backtracking to some earlier state of mind. Another point: difficulties in accepting change are not limited to changes that are thought to be undesirable. The same continuum may operate with changes that we actually want, like a new job. Given that most of us in top management both wanted and feared change, you can imagine the complex cross-currents in our psyches.

The expression of feelings induced in these workshops worked as a counter-force to the old culture. We began to see how gingerly we had treated one another, how delicately we tiptoed around areas of conflict. At least two in my group were men whom I'd worked with for 20 years. And I learnt more about them in those four days than in all the years we had spent together. That, however, was a sideshow to the main event, which was to reappraise and reconstruct the new patterns of our culture. Without this step, I now see, there would have been only a slight foundation to Benchmark. Before our work on our own behaviours and feelings, the rate of progress had been too slow.

The leadership programme was in some respects a prevention measure: to give everyone the maximum opportunity to change, and thereby to preserve as much as possible the talents and ability of the existing leadership. That is another danger of change programmes: that they stir up the waters, antagonise and demoralise, and consequently people start bailing out of the company in large numbers. Although there has been some mobility in the composition of the 130 Group, I do believe that the focus on leadership has been a powerful instrument in helping managers adjust, find their feet and increase their effectiveness. Says one who attended: 'I found that it improved our awareness of the dynamics of groups. It was difficult work. It left me drained, but there was a more focused outcome after the rough and tumble of debate.'

Drained maybe, but seminars of this type can also create a euphoria and exultation that can make participants a little 'high' and thus blind to the hard realities of implementation. We wanted to prevent the post-seminar letdown, where an individual goes to an offsite and then returns really inspired and ready to move mountains, only to find that most of the people around him are bogged down in business as usual. Consequently, we blended the learning of behavioural skills with real-world context. The core of the programme was four days of the Hamlin leadership seminar with participants who shared no organisational ties, so that they would feel safe sharing their innermost selves. 'The beauty of the programme was that it was a less threatening forum for articulating concerns and insecurities,' observes Tony Rice. 'You sat alongside colleagues, but your work team was not present – no peers, no bosses. Which meant that it was less threatening to discuss one's weaknesses.'

This phase was succeeded by an additional two-day session with members of their everyday work group, who had by then also done their four-day core behavioural workshop. The objective here was for managers to take the psychological insights gained about themselves and others, and then seek ways to change relationships and discover practices that would help them live the values in their day job. Finally, there was an additional one-day callback with the initial four-day group, designed to explore and solidify the lessons learnt.

There is a danger of holding up a change programme to a false criterion of value. For some people at BAe there was the expectation that if it were any good at all, it would have to display the functionality and dependability of an aircraft. Yet change management programmes can never have the attributes of a machine. Their processes are inexact. Progress is subtle and qualitative. There will always be great variability in different people's adjustment to and acceptance of change. One has to be philosophical about human shortcomings. Moreover, culture change requires a certain talent for extemporisation and improvisation – yet another demand that did not sit easily with our old corporate way of thinking.

Before going on this workshop, everyone in the 130 Group completed 360° feedback. This consisted of a questionnaire that an individual could send to up to 18 people – direct reports, peers and managers. The results were analysed by Hamlin and his staff, who then wrote a report rich in insights about those attitudinal and behavioural issues that the individual needed to address in the workshop setting.

Richard Lapthorne recalls: 'I was very sceptical about going on this course. I was sure that I was "too old to change". But I ended up analysing some of my own weaknesses and behaviours and over the years I could see I'd never, at any age, seriously tried to change.' But change he did, in small ways and large. As a proof, he offers the following instance of the kind of behaviour that was unimaginable in the previous culture: 'When I am directing a meeting and it comes to an end, this is what I say to everyone at the table: "When you came into the meeting you saw the agenda; you read the supporting papers. Do you believe we have had the meeting you expected to have? Are you happy with the level of discussion we had on the various issues? Are there any suggestions you can make to improve this meeting for next time?" Believe me, this approach has a massive impact.'

The goals of the Leadership Programme were to help the individual's understanding of the dynamics of change, and to deal with the barriers to his or her personal development and change responses. The sessions had the following common objectives:

⬆ Galvanise feedback from managers, colleagues, direct reports.

⬆ Analyse 'competency skills gaps' and work on removing them.

⬆ Assess interpersonal styles and understand their consequences.

⬆ Explore personal motivation and others' too.

⬆ Seek constructive ways of dealing with work-related conflict situations.

⬆ Identify personal and organisational barriers to skill development.

⬆ Develop two-way communication skills, i.e. feedback giving, active listening, influencing.

⬆ Experience confidence in self-expression.

⬆ Determine pathways to continuous learning of behaviours.

⬆ Understand how different behaviours fit into the change programme.

'This workshop was an incredible experience. For many of us it was the biggest change agent in the entire Benchmark experience,' says Steve Mogford. 'I've resolved some very difficult interpersonal situations because of it.'

Others, to be sure, had a less enthusiastic response. They experienced the programme as placing strong pressures on them to conform. To them I pointed out that we weren't looking for clonelike behaviour. There was no right way and wrong way to behave. As I see it, leaders carry the genetic code of a particular culture. Our leadership training made it clear how the code is manifest in the vision and the five values. And by so doing, it moved culture change into the very fabric of the company and changed Benchmark from a programme to the very essence of ourselves as managers – but never with a diktat. It did us in the 130 Group so much good that we used much the same materials and approaches in subsequent phases of the programme, as it spread to a larger population under the banner of BEST.

BEST

Best was the heavy canon, the Howitzer among deliverers, a sweeping education and training programme for no less than 1500 senior managers from all business units. From the very early days of Benchmark, we were acutely sensitive to what would happen as we rolled out the project to a really large number of managers and, thereafter, to the factory floor. One day we'd have to 'get real', as kids say. By mid-1996 I was itching to put Benchmark into high gear and take it at least part way to a larger population. The time had come to take a deep breath and hand the baton over to upper management, who would hereafter run with it.

I'd been warned by top managers in other companies that this moment could be our nemesis. If a significant proportion of top managers failed to buy in to the project, we would not just have to redo this portion of the project but to go back to square one, where we'd stood two years earlier. I, for one, had no stomach for that, and I'm sure nobody else in management had either. I vowed that we'd go through this phase with real intensity and care.

There was one little snag, however. The 130 Group were not enthusiastic about spreading Benchmark to others. It was the old neck of the wine bottle issue: resistance to change begins at the top. The higher-ups think that culture change will require them to give up something precious. They have a lot of knowledge of the business and they think that knowledge equates with power; so that to them sharing knowledge is the equivalent of diluting their personal power base. However, if you look below the bottleneck, into the larger volumes of people, the appetite for change gets progressively stronger further down the organisation. Many in the middle ranks are screaming for it, while everyone at the top is fighting like hell to stop it, because they foresee themselves as the losers.

According to BAe Change Manager, Peter Hawtin, 'The old BAe culture trained people to know the complete route before embarking on any kind of journey. Until they know where all the milestones are, where the petrol pumps are, they don't want to head down the motorway. Every time Dick moved to extend the franchise, it released the fear that they were going to be asked all kinds of questions by subordinates that they didn't have clear answers to.'

The reluctance of the 130 Group to let go was perhaps inevitable in any change management programme that proceeds from the centre and top of the company, then moves outwards and downwards. There was a tendency to create a 'magic circle' of those initiated into the mysteries of Benchmark. Every time I declared that we were ready to broaden the numbers of managers in the programme – from five to 20, then to 50, then 70 and thereafter expanding to the 130 Group – the magic circle said no: 'Let's keep it to ourselves awhile longer. This stuff is just too important to share.'

These symptoms were particularly acute before the launch of BEST. But I was bound and determined to move Benchmark swiftly into the ranks of upper and upper-middle management of the business units. The scale and complexity of this undertaking were considerable. The 1500 BEST participants were ten times the size of the 130 Group. 'One way or another, we've got to get our minds around this. We've got to get clarity,' I told the 130 Group in my pep talk mode. 'This is the big hurdle. I know many of you think it is about as pleasant as having a 12-inch diameter hosepipe stuck in your arm and used as an IV. But we've got to do it, and do it right.' Later in the same speech I said, 'I have benefited from the Leadership programme and learnt to express feelings. And one of the feelings I have, when I assess our progress to date, is frustration. My other emotion is excitement about coming to this milestone when we are going to push Benchmark deeper into the organisation.'

In taking Benchmark to the next level, the five values had to be presented to managers in ways that illustrated their power and their potential impact on behaviours across all types of work situations. So BAe's own change management team, supported by Mark Hamlin and Colin Price and his colleagues at Price Waterhouse, designed a group learning programme focused on each of the five values. The outcome was a string of workshops spread over 18 months that exposed 1500 managers to the skills connected to the five values. (The exposure to the people value was similar to the Leadership Training experienced by the 130 Group under Mark Hamlin.)

We sought a rigorous course that was tailored to a participant's individual needs and traits. The name we coined was Benchmark Executive Skills Training (BEST). To communicate the importance of the occasion, we exposed all BEST participants to a two-day pre-positioning event at Heathrow, in which I and other members of top management spoke of the origin and dynamics of Benchmark. Business unit managing directors all participated and spoke of their Benchmark experiences and journey to date, of the Benchmark ethos and the nature of the journey ahead of them.

BEST was not a didactic project, it was interactive. To ensure that participants got the most out of it, we went to extraordinary lengths to get them to relate the seminars to their own feelings and conduct. An important feature of this learning was the Value Plan and its relationship to the participants' work teams. We wanted participants to consider how their individual goals meshed with the goals of their natural work teams. Consequently, before the programme started we asked them to define their personal objectives and relate these to the BEST content. Participants were introduced to 360° feedback in which individuals ask subordinates, peers and supervising managers to fill in a questionnaire containing about 60 separate questions.

In some companies, 360° feedback is a bagatelle. But in the context of the emotionally reserved BAe culture, this feedback was a pretty radical departure. The idea that a person could be summed up in a collage of the views of colleagues was more than many would initially accept. Some viewed 360° feedback with the suspicion that many primitive people show to cameras, thinking that they are soul-capturing contraptions. The old BAe culture was one where people walked warily, where relentless self-justification was a common style. We now proposed that people accept workmates' criticisms without characterising them as attacks; that, in addition, they carefully listen to the observations of others and consider changing conduct if that is indicated.

Suppose, for instance, that someone was totally unaware that colleagues thought he was a remote and standoffish autocrat. He might then sit through the four days of BEST workshops on the people value, all the while thinking, 'This has nothing do with me. Not my problem at all!' By connecting the BEST training to the data from the 360° feedback, we intended to make it hard for any individual to deflect messages about values and behaviours. Thus we ensured that everyone had their own very specific value-oriented learning objectives to focus on in the course work. We didn't want people to think of BEST as some kind of sausage machine. A small point: we did not grant degrees or certificates or any emblems for BEST. The experience is the thing.

The actual content of the core BEST sessions consisted of sharing best practices from inside and outside BAe and developing competencies around each value: the tools, techniques and skills that make a particular value a living thing. In addition, the participants, who came from all over the company, shared with the others the plans of their business units, their teams' plans and their own PVPs (Personal Value Plans). This radiated an important message about us all being bound together in the one company. As with most of our Benchmark programmes, we wanted this to be an experience where there would be participant learning, not people just being talked at.

Each of the BEST candidates got a total of 12.5 days of offsite stimulus and development in less than 18 months, about as intensive an immersion as we could have, given the demands of running the business. The logistics called for bringing together large groups of roughly 100 for each of the value modules, which would be run on 15 occasions. Before and after these sessions, candidates were expected to have discussions with their work teams, so that content was linked to the practical needs of the business. Each of them went first to the module on innovation and technology, next that on partnerships, then the customer value and finally performance. The people module ran concurrently through the life of the programme as it involved a large number of small group sessions. During the programme, participants were divided into tutor groups of two dozen each – a practice copied from the 130 Group's methods. Price Waterhouse helped in the execution by providing the tutors for all but the people module, tutors for which came from Mark Hamlin's organisation. Attendees who subsequently want refreshers can obtain course material through the company's network of development centres, or by requesting CD-Roms.

BEST's cost was considerable, excluding the significant amount of work time sacrificed. Consultants, training trainers, programme administrative support and materials, hotels and travel arrangements came to significantly more than £15 million. The expense was hardly surprising, given the sheer logistical scale of the undertaking and our wish to involve so many senior managers in delivering the Benchmark messages.

In addition to deep understanding of each of the five values, and how they applied to the business, these were the traits and competencies that we expected managers to have after BEST:

⬆ Intimate understanding of the company's strategy and operational challenges.
⬆ Knowledge of the objectives and framework and their own role within Benchmark.
⬆ Skill at leading the team-based value planning process in their work environments.
⬆ Enhanced capacity to learn from others and share best practices inside and outside the company.
⬆ Trust that others can help them to learn more about themselves, via personal observation or assessment tools like 360° feedback or EFQM.
⬆ Ability to be a coach who is sensitive to people's needs and supportive of close interactions with staff.

BEST clearly paid off. We have been careful to measure the value placed by participants on their experiences at every phase of the programme. This continuous measurement enabled us to see the levels of participant satisfaction grow as the delivery of BEST unfolded. Price Waterhouse's Gerry Miles, the programme director who helped implement BEST, observed: 'Never have I seen such a powerful demonstration of commitment to a change programme as I witnessed at BAe; nor such genuine partnerships between no less than eight different business units that sent their people through BEST.'

BEST represented a point of no return. The deliberations of the 130 Group were hermetic affairs. Now Benchmark would be much more out in the open. The 130 Group no longer had control of the process, or its meanings. This represented a big psychological power shift, since now senior managers who failed to come up with the right behaviours would be readily identified by BEST graduates.

Some of the BEST candidates' early feedback was frankly critical of their superiors' conduct. They didn't see much evidence that their bosses – the same men and women who'd been at two years of quarterly meetings of the 130 Group – were living up to the values! Here are some of the negative things that BEST candidates complained about:

🔺 that colleagues in their business unit who most needed BEST wriggled out of going;
🔺 that superiors had instructed some people not to roll out the values;
🔺 that senior management of a particular business unit discouraged people from attending BEST; and the source offered to name the culprits.

One comment really got under my skin. And it was this:

🔺 'We haven't got rid of the cynics about Benchmark, and most of them are in the 130 Group.'

Imagine my dismay and anger. This accusation said that some of our top managers were two faced, behaving like lambs in the CEO workshops, but turning into non-supporters of Benchmark on their return to regular duties. This conduct may have been unconscious, but that didn't really change the effect and its damage to Benchmark. At the subsequent meeting of the 130 Group, I urged dissenters to come forward and talk to their managers and seek help, or alternatively to find employment in another company. Our entire culture change programme was predicated on role modelling as the chief instrument of communication and dissemination. This feedback indicated that appropriate role modelling was just not happening to the degree required.

I asked the 130 Group to debate this issue. What were their ideas for the shortfalls in role modelling the values? God knows, I pointed out, we'd discussed and hammered away at them for nigh on two years. Clearly, something more was needed. But what? The solution they came up with was perfectly in accord with the spirit of Benchmark: henceforth, we'd measure and score behaviours of members of the 130 Group according to how well they lived up to the values. Everyone thought this was a great idea in the abstract. But when it came time to implement it, there was widespread apprehension and fear.

This piece of Benchmark is called Peer Group Assessment. Colin Price will describe it in detail when he talks about measurement in Chapter 9. So far as I know, nothing like it has been adopted in the really senior ranks of any British company. In Peer Group Assessment everyone in top management is rated by about 30 peers, not with vague descriptive language about good and bad traits, but with hard scores against an array of attributes based on the values. And when the results were announced, most of those who scored poorly were literally stunned by the results. In some cases we actually offered them counselling services to help them cope. Peer Group Assessment was one of the hardest things undertaken by the 130 Group, but there is no doubt in my mind that it helped people understand the objective impact of their conduct and hence made them better able to role model Benchmark values.

This said, I also took the charge of cynicism in the 130 Group with a pinch of salt. When judging our superiors, it is human nature to magnify their shortcomings and imperfections. And in a change programme like ours, even managers with 100 per cent best intentions to modify their conduct could only do so slowly – as I knew from my own case. Then, too, there were instances where managers really had changed their conduct but subordinates were not about to give them the credit. As one BEST participant said of his boss: 'Either he is going for an Oscar, or he's changed!', leaving the impression that the latter possibility was most unlikely.

Feedback from BEST has been increasingly positive, as we have refined and focused the delivery. Here are some more positive comments from recent participants:

↑ 'We change or die, and this programme shows how.'
↑ 'I had no idea before this that our company could be so creative.'
↑ 'I feel that now I can do something positive.'
↑ 'Keep the support and momentum going, please.'
↑ 'It has considerably reinforced the development areas I am interested in.'

A doctoral student from Lancaster University, Sharon Turnbull, participated in several BEST sessions and interviewed over 75 participants. Her conclusion: 'The BEST programme has raised considerable hope amongst this population, and optimism that the company can succeed in creating a culture where the sharing of best practices is encouraged; where old rivalries begin to disappear; where creativity and risk are encouraged; and where participation rather than control and listening rather than shouting become the norm.'

Speaking of the BEST people module, John Weston has observed: 'BEST made us confront a lot of difficult stuff, a lot of scary stuff. It forced most of us to move out of our comfort zones and to consider psychological dimensions of our behaviour and to look at ourselves, and our peers, in ways that we'd never dared look before.'

Because of the large emotional and financial investment in BEST, the top management of the company demanded pretty rigorous measures of its impact. Key facets of BEST were continuously assessed and reported monthly to the operations committee, which I chaired. From where we sat, we could see that BEST recorded a solid pattern of improvement as the programme found its legs and focus. Initially BEST was predominantly a domestic affair, but it was then expanded and slightly reconfigured for local conditions in BAe sites in France, Germany, the US, Australia and Saudi Arabia.

Team Leader Training

In an earlier chapter I described the Value Plan as one of the important catalytic actions for the performance value. This process entailed a complex, bottom-up planning exercise, in which the master corporate plan consisted of modules drawn up by the business units and by the teams within them. The basic building block of the entire process is the individual within a team, meaning that the realisation of the plan critically depends on how that individual perceives the near- and far-term opportunities for improvement in value-based conduct. In this way, the Value Plan is designed to do some heavy lifting for Benchmark.

The programme that would drive Benchmark beyond BEST we dubbed Team Leader Training. Its goal is to help people improve how they work and interact, and to follow this up with a team plan to deliver these improvements. As a key supporter of this process, the Performance Value Team helped create a team leader workbook, designed to orient and to instruct the user on how to create team-based Value Plans with some simple procedures. It can be used in various ways: as a manual, or merely a checklist for the teams. Similar kinds of aids have been used in other companies, including British Airways.

Value planning provides the mechanism for harnessing the collective will, ideas and talent of our people. The broad goals of team-based value planning are as follows:

➤ Clarify the objectives and targets given to the teams by the corporate, business unit or departmental Value Plan. All team plans are subsumed under and aligned with these larger plan frameworks.

↑ Audit the team's current performance against the five values, via objective criteria – from EFQM surveys, employee attitude surveys, customer assessments.

↑ Set improvement targets.

↑ Share the plan with the rest of the organisation, so that best practice sharing can occur.

↑ Regularly review progress, or lack of it, against the Value Plan goals.

Involvement is a key attribute of a team-based Value Plan. It is not the output of a leader dictating terms, but the result of the combined contribution of the team. The leader is the coach and the scout. Team-based Value Plans avoid the flaw of so many traditional planning mechanisms: the tendency to create wishlists that cannot guide realistic decision making. Teams are given wide latitude in setting goals. They are free to challenge targets in the light of shifts in external environments, to make them more or less ambitious. The one thing that is inflexible is that the plan must act as a framework that links the individual to the company as a whole, the team to the business unit, and the business unit to the centre plan.

So much for the Value Plan machinery. How does Team Leader Training (TLT) fit in with it? It is actually something of a misnomer, because:

↑ in fact it doesn't train people to be team leaders, and

↑ it isn't directed only at those with 'team leader' painted on their office doors, but available for anyone in the company who has a leadership role.

TLT is a major transmission vehicle for delivery of Benchmark to all employees. It does this by in effect creating a nucleus, a concentration of the values in the persons of the leaders, who receive two days of training. About 5000 people are scheduled for this experience over the next two years.

Although I have said that the greatest resistance to change is at the top of the organisation and that middle managers welcome it, this is somewhat of a simplification. In reality, change releases ambivalence. There are always reasons for embracing or rejecting it. We were aware that many in the population targeted for Team Leader Training had a big investment in the status quo, a set of expectations that were the fruit of long immersion in the old culture.

'If you go down the layers of management in sequence, you eventually come to the group leader, a layer that is very populous in the engineering area,' says David Gardner, Director of Engineering. 'Typically a group leader will have spent between 15 and 20 years working his way up from the bottom, into a position where he has about 20 people working for him directly: some authority, a little area that he can call his own. And along comes somebody and says, "Right, we are going to change all that, and by the way we are disbanding the group leader role: instead we're moving everyone from specialist functions into project functions." This manager is left sitting there, head in his hands, thinking, "It's taken me 20 years to get into a position of authority, and suddenly it's gone, and they are asking me to buy into that."'

To combat this discouragement, we would have to train leaders to be the champions and communicators of Benchmark. By word and deed, they would help implant the five values and the Value Plan into the fabric of the team's deliberations, interactions and decision making. The actual TLT curriculum deals with the techniques of running productive participatory meetings, presentation and leadership skills, the psychology of team effectiveness and of mature business conduct, the art of listening and questioning and problem solving. Other modules that are available to team leaders focus on coaching skills, lean manufacturing and process modelling. We haven't sought standardisation: leaders in each business unit freely adopt those modules that meet their needs.

Virtual University

Corporate universities have appeared in good number in the last decade, notably in the US. Many of them offer little more than quickie employee training and skill-booster programmes. Some aspire to be much more than that: to truly enhance the knowledge and performance bases of the firm. Some of the better-known names in the field include GE, IBM, Ford Motor, Motorola, Dana Corp., Eddie Bauer, the US Patent Office, General Motors' Saturn Division. Needless to say, there are many corporate training and education programmes that are effective higher knowledge builders that do not operate under the university concept or name.

For BAe, the concept of a university without walls seemed particularly apt. By this means we might achieve some really important goals, such as:

⬆ Improve our skills and knowledge and so increase workforce competencies.
⬆ Enhance knowledge and stimulate the sharing of best practices between business units, and between ourselves and suppliers and customers.
⬆ Advance our internal benchmarking capabilities by creating uniform knowledge-based systems and programmes across all business units.
⬆ Bring under one roof the divisions' more than 60 alliances with academia, also their professional and management development efforts and apprenticeship programmes.
⬆ Further the culture change initiatives under Benchmark by fostering unity and corporate identity.
⬆ Improve our image among and intake of quality recruits, since the Virtual University is a window through which the external world can see the company at its best.

This is a very far-reaching agenda. It is perhaps the most ambitious corporate university in the UK. It is also a major investment, likely to cost more than £1 billion over the coming decade. The university, launched in April 1998, has three faculties, each with ties to outside institutions: an Engineering and Manufacturing Technology faculty, an International Business School, and a Learning Faculty. In addition, there is a Benchmarking and Best

Practice Centre, which will for the first time create structures and processes to break the logjams that bedevil the exchange of fertile and good ideas and procedures within BAe. In order to emphasise the central role of the BAe Virtual University, we have placed the company's Sowerby Research Centre, located outside Bristol, within the university's non-existent walls.

BAe annually makes very significant investments in its people's skills and knowledge. For example, in 1997 we spent a total of £34 million on off-the-job training, without counting salary costs or the hundreds of on-the-job training efforts. The Virtual University will focus and add value to the training and education investment. Another achievement of the Virtual University has been to pull together into a single network the major Learning Centres at different business units. The network now delivers a large spectrum of learning opportunities to every employee who seeks them.

I sometimes think we at BAe are a little obsessed with the possibilities of best practice sharing. If so, it is an obsession that we have in common with others. Lew Pratt, CEO of Hewlett-Packard, has said, I imagine in a wishful tone, 'If HP knew what HP knows, we would be three times more profitable.' A steady flow of best practice sharing was always one of the anticipated deliverables from Benchmark and we've started to see some results at last. The best practice unit has conducted forums on capturing and sharing knowledge within BAe, as well as forging links to many outsider repositories of best practice at home and abroad – most of these currently available on our intranet clearing house of best-practice data.

Dr Geraldine Kenney-Wallace, Managing Director and Vice-Chancellor of the Virtual University, says that the goal of the best practice unit is to 'Catalyse it. Find it. Share it.' People can volunteer a best practice to the centre, or they can ask centre personnel to locate knowledge for them, either outside or in other parts of BAe. Sharing can yield some pretty quick gains. For instance, we found that four different business units purchased the identical high-end software package. Consequently, we've begun to rationalise procurement and get duplication out of the business units' licensing agreements.

Here is a story illustrating the kind of best-practice interchange that if were it echoed again and again through the company would yield massive bottom-line improvement. In 1996 some middle managers in the Military Aircraft Division did some freelance scouting for best manufacturing practices within BAe for the Mid-Life Upgrade (MLU) of the Tornado fighter. They were looking for a system for parts packaging and display that the mechanics working on the planes could access. Previously there had been no system: the parts were plucked out of inventory and put into a plastic bag, which the mechanic working on the plane would dip into, like a large bag of potato chips.

The state-of-the-art solution to this problem consisted of foam-backed suitcases, with parts being placed into scooped areas in the foam. However, the project manager, based at Warton outside Preston, was curious to learn about other sites' experience with the suitcase. He checked with Chester, a site for commercial aviation, and found that they had evolved a different method, in which parts were shrinkwrapped to a piece of cardboard. This was in some ways superior to the suitcase and a lot cheaper, so it was adopted at Warton.

Over the life of the MLU programme, the shrinkwrap approach should yield over £300,000 in materials economies. If the same method were applied to the full production run on the Eurofighter, estimated savings could be over £6 million. And in the case of Nimrod, the economies using this process, on which BAe has obtained a patent, will again be substantial. This case vividly illustrates what we are trying to accelerate and expand with the best practice centre.

Programme infrastructure

There are three *dramatis personae* in a change management programme:

⬆ the strategists, who see the external market threats and opportunities and craft the visions and the values;

⬆ the technicians, who in the background work out the programme designs, the tools, the workshops, the learning and communication tools;

⬆ the receivers and adopters of the change message.

This part of my story is about the second group who, so far as I can see in many change programmes, are rarely acknowledged and given the credit they deserve.

Up to now I have spoken of the motives for Benchmark, the intentions, the ideology. Now we discuss machinery and techniques of execution. Culture change is a highly complex activity, as I'm sure readers will have grasped by now. No programme can expect to succeed without a high level of expertise in the technologies of change, backed by staff and infrastructure that has a lot of credibility with the rest of the company. In this regard, I was fortunate to find and pick Colin Price as the primary outside adviser.

In addition to Colin Price, we had a full-time internal consulting group headed by Peter Hawtin, who had previously worked on change management initiatives at the Rover Group and at our Royal Ordnance division. Peter at first worked under Rob Meakin, the first Benchmark head who subsequently left us to be human resource boss at GEC. Meakin really was the ship's pilot in the early days as senior managers dipped their toes in the unfamiliar waters of culture change. Peter's small team was staffed with promising line managers, who passed through on a rotational basis every year or so, returning to their business units to help disseminate Benchmark. Peter and his team knew the complex chemistries that are released by change efforts and they had a deep network of personal contacts in the business units where the real transformation had to take place. They anticipated managers' reactions to various initiatives, fought fires, understood company politics, interpreted feedback and found remedies for aspects of the programme that were going off the rails.

The internal consulting team also provided skills in staging the various top management meetings, the 130 Group and its predecessors. It was essential that the participants came away from these events ready to invest further personal time and energy in Benchmark. There were a couple of occasions in the early days when, frankly, it was touch and go as to whether the group would buy into the project. Peter's skills at impression management were invaluable. 'In the first twelve months things were pretty fragile. I do think we could have blown it if we'd had one bad workshop,' he said. Failing to win them over at this point could have had very serious consequences.

A lot of attention was paid to the staging of these gatherings. We used very good-quality hotels and conference facilities. Though it would have been more economical, we did not use one of the many company sites where we had equivalent facilities. This would have sent a parochial and therefore wrong message. We hired stimulating speakers and outside presenters. I personally signed all the invitations and Peter arranged the seating in ways that fostered fruitful interactions and defused potential frictions among the attendees. Casual dress was *de rigueur*, to convey the message that people should relax, let their hair down.

Change implementation on the cheap is a bad idea. Messages lose focus. Momentum is dissipated. Underresourcing the project runs the risk that the forces that stand opposed to change are not really engaged and disarmed. There were some in top management who thought that we should have a cost–benefit appraisal of Benchmark. I thought that would be a dead end. Once you get into bean counting on something like this you will always find reasons for diluting its quality. And quality is axiomatic in a project designed to make us benchmark. So we went first class, and thereby also conveyed to everyone the seriousness of the undertaking.

There is also the question of tempo and intensity. Change does not run on automatic. It needs to be galvanised, directed, fine-tuned. Successive meetings of top managers had to cover new ground, convey a sense of purpose, build critical mass. For example, the meetings of the 130 Group were pretty didactic in the beginning. In response to popular demand, we began to structure them so that people were given more learning opportunities in each of the five values.

To further underline the centrality of Benchmark, we went to all the business units and identified 15 of their top, up-and-coming young managers from each. These were seconded to Benchmark, to work as facilitators and staff support to each of the five value teams. Since we took the cream of the business units' talents, the members of the 130 Group finally saw the light and said, 'We think this guy's serious.'

One of my headline-making moves was the appointment of Rob Meakin's successor to head up Benchmark. At that juncture, Benchmark had been running for about 18 months and I seriously worried that it did not have enough lift. We needed to get more senior managers off the fence and signed on. The feedback I got was that many of them perceived Benchmark as predominantly an art form for the personnel department. The personnel department's lack of authority could be used by members of the 130 Group as a pretext for not getting serious about the project. I feared that there was creeping inertia, which if unchecked would dilute and eventually destroy. Something had to be found to put fire in their bellies.

So I took one of the senior 'barons' of our business, the managing director of Military Aircraft, Kevin Smith, and put him in charge of Benchmark. That had a tremendous impact on everyone. Kevin's was widely seen as the most important job in the company. Evidently, the fact that I'd been giving up 30 per cent of my time to Benchmark did not seem to have had the same impact on the troops.

'The appointment of Kevin Smith was very, very significant,' says Damien Turner, Managing Director – Consultancy Services, at our Systems & Services Division. 'Perhaps it was the biggest single thing in the programme – to take the man who was running the largest part of the business and say that this culture change programme is so important that it merits this guy's undivided focus. That carried an awful lot of weight.'

As I'd anticipated, Kevin galvanised Benchmark, giving it considerable focus and backbone in his one year at the helm. He was succeeded in 1997 by another highly praised operations manager, Terry Morgan, our present Director of Human Resources. Terry has done sterling work in expanding the Benchmark franchise and enthusiastically maintaining the project's tempo as it has rolled out to a larger population.

Communications

Our communications objective was to beam culture change deeply into the organisation. Our habit of always looking at issues through the prism of behaviour meant that our communications efforts could not be simply evangelical, they had to have nitty-gritty behavioural consequences. As Colin Price notes elsewhere in this book, bombastic change programmes that use fanfares, pronouncements, slogans etc. quickly raise expectations. Everyone gets wildly enthusiastic, but the buzz soon fades and disillusionment quickly sets in.

My first communication to the bulk of the workforce about Benchmark was in 1995, during one of my periodic videos for distribution to employees. In it I outlined the increasingly difficult competitive environment and declared that the only remedy was to be a benchmark company across the board. A year later I unveiled the five values to everyone in the company, and explained their meanings in a subsequent employee video. In 1996 we created the first ever corporate employee publication, called *Arrow*, which comes out six times a year and extensively covers Benchmark developments.

In June 1997 we held a one-day meeting in Blackpool to communicate Benchmark to a broad cross-section of some 1500 employees. The largest pan-BAe group ever assembled was taken to the Winter Gardens in Blackpool, where we staged a powerful presentation of the Benchmark message, beginning with the competitive challenge, the vision and the five values and the reasons behind them. Though it was a successful unveiling, we decided that future communications should be more concretely linked to inducing direct behaviour change.

Communications were fundamental to all facets of Benchmark. From the quarterly meetings of the 130 Group to BEST and Team Leader Training, we constantly worried how to communicate and target the vision, the values, the competitive framework. In other words, communication was integrated to the deliverables of behaviour change. 'This was quite different from most change programmes,' Peter Hawtin notes. 'We communicated to the vast majority of the employees on the back of an operational activity and not, as is so often the case, on the back of a communications activity.'

Strategic Leaders Programme

This was a skill-enhancement and consciousness-boosting exercise for key players within the 130 Group. The goal: to ensure the highest level of competence in present and future leadership of the company. In the training and development field there are literally thousands of top-flight senior executive programmes for sale. However, none that we looked at had all the ingredients we sought, chief of which was to provide our leaders with a global perspective, as befits a company with 85 per cent of revenues stemming from overseas and a participant in numerous foreign partnerships. Although the record demonstrates that BAe is hardly an insular organisation, we felt the need to extend the range of our knowledge of, and insights about, global socioeconomic conditions, present and to come. So we built our own programme, tailored to these requirements, which ended up with five days of training and best-practice sharing in different parts of the world – assisted by prominent local business schools in France, India, China and the US.

Like the various actions I described in Chapter 6, these deliverers have been of first-class quality. Most readers will have noted that they are all geared to 'hearts and minds' issues, or 'passion and brain' – they attempt to help managers change behaviour through learning and conditioning. I suppose one might argue that the number and intensity of these deliverers could be a case of overkill. But any culture change programme takes big chances if it underestimates the difficulties of changing behaviour. Somewhere in the course of the change journey there is an invisible line drawn across the road, equal to the point at which more than half of all top managers in business units have made credible efforts to change ways of thought and conduct. It is at this moment that, finally, the programme has a good shot at success. Failure to reach this point almost guarantees failure. Underinvesting in the deliverers was therefore a risk we could not take.

Up to now I have written the chapters that advance the narrative and left Colin Price to follow up with some more cerebral observations about culture change. In the next chapter there will be a change of roles. He will take up the rather thorny issues of measuring progress in culture change and how we at BAe attempted to solve them. I will follow him with a summary of some key Benchmark achievements.

Dear Dick

I believe that with the measures that we are now beginning to put in place – balanced scorecard, peer recognition etc. – we are beginning to make real progress. We need to keep the Value Teams in place to ensure that the momentum we have built up is not lost.

***

Dear Dick

Since the workshop, I have also spent time at the pilot module of BEST Partnerships, and my experience there reinforces the message. If you gather together a small group of our people away from their work environment and pressures to discuss the generalities or the specifics of our business, they will do so in a cooperative and non-BU political manner and with BAe's interests to the fore. They relate to each other as human beings, not as bearers of tribal regalia. It is also clear that they have no illusions about the scene within BAe and in general they want to be part of fixing the problems, not perpetuating them.

***

Dear Dick

There are many positive changes coming from Benchmark, but I am starting to worry that we are recreating a hierarchy, the 130 Group, the 1500 (BEST) group, then a larger group, some of whom (but not all) went to Blackpool, then a still larger group not really picked up by anything. We need to break down 'them & us' and status type barriers. Instead we seem to be creating them and enforcing them.

***

Dear Dick

I was just a little concerned about the emphasis placed upon getting 'everybody involved in the Business Plan and using this as a means of communication. Firstly, I think it is impractical to get all 46,000 involved and most will not buy into the concept that this is actually driving change. Secondly, the financial information contained within the plans are market sensitive and thus cannot be broadcast.

***

Dear Dick

For the first time I see us coming together as a company. We have had terrific exchanges of views in these meetings and recognised some fundamental problems that need to be corrected.

***

Dear Dick

In terms of workshop content I felt the team did an excellent job in translating the difficult concepts around Technology and Innovation into something meaningful and tangible. However, I did get into data overload and have to admit that energy levels did drain and concentration was lost on a number of occasions. I believe we had approximately 15 presentations during the day and I would question if this is digestible in this form.

***

Dear Dick

I believe that the power of a programme such as this has to be in all 46,000 employees within the company being participants. The behaviours and practices will therefore have to be easily understood and applicable to the mass population rather than sections of the company.

***

Dear Dick

We should think very carefully before we adapt any 'sheep dip' approach to providing tools; we've tried it before and it hasn't worked. You first of all have to create the environment in which tools can be deployed effectively, and deliver them to where they are needed, which may not be everywhere.

***

Dear Dick

I would support the EFQM proposal. It is a good framework, and it would be more useful if it was consistently applied across the company. I did notice a few people shaking their heads, when a group-wide approach was first suggested. But as discussion progressed, none of them spoke out. This might have been a significant watershed, to see divisional 'barons' bowing to peer group pressure that advocated the clearly better group-wide approach. Then again maybe it won't be a watershed if they adopt their traditional style and quietly obstruct the idea outside the meeting.

***

Dear Dick

The Employee Opinion Survey and the Business Excellence Review have both now provided valuable feedback on progress in all the important areas. Overall they seem to be showing some encouraging trends. We clearly, however, have a long way to go with the actions we have identified – particularly in the areas of leadership and customer satisfaction. 'Keep pressing on at all levels', that for me remains the key message.

***

Dear Dick

May I suggest that for us all leadership skills is a huge but, in my view, absolutely necessary action. I would also make a plea that we try not to get too sophisticated too quickly. I totally support 360° appraisal, and I have used it in previous companies. But doing the appraisal is the easy bit. Taking the actions that follow can be complex and hugely time-consuming.

Dear Dick

My concerns are on the implementations side. Are the aims Utopian? Is there a danger of a scatter-gun approach? Can we really involve 46,000 people in the business planning process, or are we kidding ourselves? Perhaps more importantly, do the 46,000 want to be involved?

***

Dear Dick

Shortly after the workshop I attended the BEST Customer Module as a delegate. I was very impressed by the enthusiasm and commitment shown by the BEST participants, and by the quality of the tutoring. Not only was the content (tools and techniques) professionally taught, but the whole event buzzed in a way that really reinforced the positive messages of Benchmark BAe.

9
WHAT GETS MEASURED GETS DONE

All corporations have been frustrated at the difficulties of measurement in a culture change programme. Many simply give up trying to measure with any rigour or consistency. It is easy to see why. There are so many intangibles, feedback loops and abstract totems like 'quality' or 'customer service' for which there are no 100 per cent reliable sensing devices. However, if a management gives in to this frustration, it is very likely to damage the legitimacy of the programme. In business reality is primarily captured with measurement, with data, with trends, audit trails etc. Culture change programmes won't last long if they are only sanctioned by subjective criteria, such as support from the chief executive or from the HR boss. They must find credible measures of change.

Such measurement does not have to be watertight, far less adhere to 'generally accepted accounting principles'. And if the measures are indirect, or fuzzy, or a bit wobbly at the start of the programme, experimentation and experience will most likely improve them. I know of no company that has tackled this issue with more determination and such powerful results as BAe. BAe's measurements fall into three overlapping categories: progress, effects and benefits.

Progress

The issue addressed here is whether or not we have done the things that we set out to do. It's surprising how many change programmes lack rigour and fail to apply those project management disciplines that companies readily apply to other initiatives, such as new product introductions and new facility building. This is a grave mistake. Such deviations from normal practice leave the programme vulnerable to criticism that it is some flaky activity on the side.

The culture change programme at BAe has been held to the highest standards of project management; understandably, given that the goal was to be the benchmark in every way possible. If a change programme espouses speed, focus and performance orientation, then the programme itself needs to be implemented in accordance with these principles.

Progress was primarily tracked at BAe with the Benchmark Success Board, a simple matrix that shows where each of the main divisions (headquarters is a division for these purposes) stands in terms of fulfilling every one of the many actions that support the five values. There are four points of demarcation on the scale. An action at a business unit can:

↑ have no plan (or be at some major variance to plan);
↑ have slipped against the plan;
↑ be on target;
↑ or be not yet in deployment.

Each of these measures is kept up to date and results posted on the intranet. 'The idea is to provide a snapshot of how each division is performing in adopting the actions,' says Terry Morgan. 'It is not a stick to beat people up with, nor a league table that should spur competition between business units. It is meant to be a reality check. Are you doing what you said you'd do?'

The Success Board is periodically reviewed by Dick Evans and other members of the leadership team. This guarantees that there will be laser-like focus on progress against milestones and an implementation schedule that the business units themselves set. The Success Board has yet another benefit. It enables management to see which of the five values are getting fulfilled in actions and which are struggling. (Most of the actions on the table, but not all, are described in detail by Dick Evans in Chapter 6.)

Benchmark success board
Benchmark values in action

	Military Aircraft & Aerospace	Royal Ordnance	RA	Airbus	Head Office	BAe Asset Management	Systems & Services	BAe Systems & Equipment
Customer care policy	○	●	⊗	○	○	○	⊗	○
Self-assessment tool	○	●	●	◍	●	○	●	○
OSI links to reward and recognition	○	○	●	○	○	○	●	○
Training and development	○	●	●	○	◍	●	●	○
Leadership development	◍	●	●	⊗	◍	◍	◍	◍
Personal development plan	◍	◍	◍	◍	◍	◍	●	◍
Involvement scheme	◍	⊗	◍	⊗	◍	◍	●	◍
Value plan	◍	◍	◍	◍	◍	◍	●	◍
Value based management	⊗	⊗	○	⊗	●	⊗	●	◍
Business excellence review	◍	⊗	◍	◍	◍	◍	●	◍
Intranet	◍	●	◍	◍	⊗	◍	⊗	◍
Process for innovation	○	◍	○	●	○	○	○	○
Benchmark culture industrial partnerships	○	●	○	○	◍	◍	○	●
Partnership personal policy	○	●	○	⊗	◍	○	○	○
Champion for collaboration	⊗	⊗	◍	◍	⊗	⊗	◍	◍
Supplier partnership	◍	◍	◍	◍	◍	⊗	◍	◍

○ Not yet at deployment stage   ⊗ Slippage against plan

◍ Deployment plan on target   ● No plan/major variance to plan

Effects

The effects of culture change are much harder to judge than progress against timetables, simply because culture is so diffuse. BAe used two excellent measures to gauge the degree of culture shift:

↑ opinion surveys;
↑ the peer review process within the 130 Group.

Employee opinion sampling is a fairly well-accepted technique in modern management. In the course of a culture change exercise, it is essential for it to be done frequently and as thoroughly as possible to capture the vectors of culture change – in BAe's case the degree to which the five values have taken hold. This said, we have to recognise that culture change often operates at a glacial speed; massive inputs and interventions at the top of the funnel spread only slowly into group consciousness. The conclusion should be obvious: companies should not expect to see culture change reflected in large swings in employee perceptions. Relatively small gains are most likely.

Prior to Benchmark, the various business units had conducted periodic opinion surveys but (no surprise!) these were largely incompatible with each other. This made interpreting the results across the company very difficult. In 1995, BAe conducted a baseline corporate-wide survey, which was followed by another in December 1997 of 21,000 employees at all 11 main facilities. The two strongest findings were that two-thirds of workers were satisfied with their jobs and expected still to be working for the company three years hence. This was certainly encouraging, considering how low morale had been three years earlier.

Measures of the vitality of the values also produced good news:

Customers 80 per cent said: 'I strive to exceed my customers' expectations.'

People 80 per cent said: 'I am trusted to make my own decisions within the company.'

Partnership 73 per cent said: 'Development of open, honest relationships with partners and joint ventures will improve BAe's performance.'

Innovation and technology 46 per cent said: 'Developing ideas that may deliver benefits to my business unit is encouraged.'

But when the study compared some key employee responses with external benchmarks of a cluster of companies polled by the Gallup Organisation, the BAe results were still far behind the pack. Here are some of the questions on which benchmark remained a pretty distant dream:

↑ I have the materials and equipment I need to do my work well.
↑ I have the opportunity to do what I do best.
↑ I know what they expect of me.
↑ In the last seven days I have been recognised or praised for good work.
↑ My immediate management/team leader seems to care about me as a person.
↑ My immediate management/team leader encourages my development.
↑ In my business unit my opinions seem to count.
↑ The vision of the company makes me feel my job is important.

There was one area where BAe employees exceeded the Gallup benchmark, in answer to the question: 'My fellow employees are committed to doing quality work.' This is further evidence of what is perhaps BAe's deepest single ethic, and the one quality that allowed it to survive the debacle of 1991–92: engineering and technical competence. So it would have been astonishing if the opinion sample had shown anything different.

Self-criticism is one of the best characteristics of the BAe culture. It was therefore quite in character for management to review the 1997 data and set goals and targets for future surveys. In mid-1998 there was a random check of the opinions of some 1000 employees, which showed improvements in three-quarters of the questions in the earlier survey. Some really big gains were recorded on the following issues, an astonishing result and a real validation of our efforts:

↑ In the last six months, my immediate manager/team leader has talked to me about my progress.

⬆ Innovation is truly encouraged.

⬆ In the last month I have been encouraged to think of ways to improve performance.

⬆ In my business unit my opinions seem to count.

⬆ My immediate manager/team leader has helped me understand who my customers are.

The second thing that British Aerospace did to test the value shift was to introduce its Peer Recognition Process to the 130 Group, to get a picture of how far top executive behaviour corresponded with the five values. Readers may recall that in the previous chapter Dick Evans was dismayed to find evidence coming from managers at an immediately lower level to the 130 Group that their superiors were not living the values, and some seemed to be actively undermining them. The remedy chosen was characteristic of BAe – measurement. But before there is measurement, there first has to be clarity about exactly what behaviours are desirable and not desirable in terms of realising the values. BAe has done impressive work in this area. As an illustration of the detail and thoroughness of its behaviour definition, look at the Behaviour Recognition Matrix on the next page.

When talking about peer recognition, BAe managers unconsciously lower their voices. Their sombre tone indicates awe and amazement that they have come so far from the moorings of the old culture. 'Peer group assessment was a hell of a difficult issue,' Dick Evans has said. 'In discussion everyone subscribed to it. But when it came to actually doing it, people found it traumatic. And some were completely taken aback by their results.' He adds, 'This was one of the most difficult things that the 130 Group had to face up to. I promised them if it turned out to be counter-productive we'd not do it again, but meanwhile let's see if we can't learn something out of this process.'

Peer recognition called for all members of the 130 Group to score others along the behavioural parameters in the matrix. Individuals got input from around 20 other managers – mostly via the intranet, but some with paper. (The lowest number of reviews

	Customer	People	Innovation & Technology	Performance	Partnership
6 Role model	• Acts as a trusted adviser, helping customers to determine their requirements and expectations • Investigates and offers alternative solutions to delight the customer	• Treats everyone as an equal and is sensitive to different perspectives and aspirations • Encourages the team to work together and utilises their skills and talents • Builds working relationships with external teams	• Acts as a champion for innovation and change both inside and outside of their discipline • Creates business processes in order to gain the most value from innovation • Continually generates viable ideas and suggestions that are new to British Aerospace and to the industry	• An outstanding achiever for whom measurement, benchmarking and continuous improvement are second nature • Inspires, challenges and motivates others • Always celebrates successes and aims to be the best	• Displays an outstanding ability to work with partners for the benefit of the partnership, and British Aerospace as a whole • Respects their needs and shares information freely • Strives for the achievement of the common goals
5 Positive contributor	• Inspires confidence in the development of strategies to ensure long-term customer delight • Builds open, honest and lasting relationships with customers • Identifies, monitors and responds promptly to customers' concerns • Has introduced jointly agreed measures to monitor performance	• Listens and is sensitive to the opinions of others • Creates a culture in which personal development is seen as the norm • Builds on the strength of team members and recognises when they need support	• Creates an environment where innovation and change are welcomed and takes active steps to bring them about • Monitors the progress of new ideas against a strategy for change and improvement • Actively drives change within the team	• Achieves a lot – usually more than expected • Creates a positive working environment • Frequently celebrates successes • Reviews progress against stretching targets and makes good use of benchmarking to improve performance	• Builds long-term relationships based on honest and open communication • Has introduced jointly agreed measures to monitor performance • Holds regular reviews to identify areas for improvement
4 Contributor	• Measures customer satisfaction by seeking, sharing and acting on feedback • Anticipates customers' needs may change and looks beyond their immediate demands • Regularly reviews performance • Encourages others to adopt the same high standards	• Makes a valued contribution to the team • Puts time and effort into their development and encourages others to do the same • Is honest and open with colleagues	• Frequently produces ideas externally to their job and implements them • Adopts change initiatives enthusiastically and effectively • Regular and effective user of IT • Identifies, monitors and responds to the impact of technology	• Meets all targets and deadlines • Maintains a high standard of work • Draws on benchmarking and continuous improvement techniques • Applies some measures to monitor performance	• Works closely with their partners and adapts well to their changing needs and expectations • Regularly reviews performance measures
3 Occasional contributor	• Knows who their customers are and what they require • Is unable to build trusting relationships with customers • Makes an effort to monitor their performance with customers	• Has an understanding of people's needs but requires further development to assist them • Is often influenced by others and open to persuasion • Wants to develop personally but not always motivated to do so	• Is creative within the parameters of their own arena • Carries out some sharing and implementing of best practice • Recognises the need to change	• Meets most targets and deadlines, but not always • Occasionally draws on best practice to bring about improvements • Quality of work is usually of an acceptable standard	• Attempts to keep partners up to date with progress • Responds to requests in an ad hoc manner • Some performance measures agreed
2 Inconsistent contributor	• Is more or less aware of what the customer requires but does not always act on their needs • Makes an effort to monitor performance • Fails to measure customer satisfaction	• Attempts to encourage team working • Displays little interest in personal development • Fails to thank others for their help	• Creates some new ideas but fails to implement them • Fails to encourage their team to come up with improvement ideas • Does not recognise the need to change	• Occasionally meets targets and deadlines • Shows no desire for achievement • Will accept poor quality of work from their team • Does not always celebrate success	• Values some partnerships, but fails to work effectively with all of them • Fails to agree performance measures with their partners • Limited contact made with their partners
1 Negative contributor	• Does not recognise who their customers are • Fails to identify customer needs • Does not encourage others to do the best for the customer	• Does not react appropriately to the feelings and behaviours of others • Is unreliable and lacks trust • Fails to assist in development of their team	• Fails to challenge traditional ways of working • Reluctant to learn how technology could improve their performance • Is not open to new ideas and concepts	• Fails to meet targets and deadlines • Quality of work is poor • Shows no interest in improving their own performance or that of the team • Fosters a negative atmosphere at work	• Does not want to create partnerships as sees no value in them • Fails to identify the roles, activities and concerns of their partners

for anyone was seven, the highest 40.) The responses were added up to a numerical score for each individual against each of the five values, plus an overall score. Participants were also given comparative data on where the group as a whole scored along the behaviour continuum. With the results mailed in confidence to participants, each was given names and phone numbers of four external people ready to offer counselling.

Individual scores on any one value could range up to an exemplary 6 for anyone deemed a perfect role model. Actual scores ranged from a low of 3.08 to a high of 5.05. Looked at in a normal distribution curve, most came out somewhere in the middle. There were 15 in the top-scoring group and 14 in the bottom, who were not living the values to an obvious degree. 'When the results came in they gave Dick Evans and others in the high command an important tool in evaluating people for promotion,' says Peter Hawtin. 'It is still an immature tool: when we get it to work better we will percolate it down to the rest of the company.'

There were feelings in the 130 group that this part of the programme smacked of Big Brother. People imagined colleagues they'd had differences with now sitting in front of their computer terminal anonymously settling old quarrels by dishing out scores of 1s, 2s and 3s. At the end of this chapter there are phrases from a number of 'Letters to Dick' expressing criticism of the Peer Review Process, which I think most human beings would share to some degree. Against this has to be weighed the centrality of behavioural change to the success of Benchmark. Failure was certain unless a spur was applied to the behaviour of the top guys. In the end, Dick Evans' character, the man's evident personal decency, helped peer assessment win acceptance. It's interesting to note that most of those who came at the bottom of the scoring range have left the organisation, pretty much of their own volition.

In the event, 120 managers scored between 3.8 and 4.5, such a favourable skew that – I did say, remember, they're a really self-critical crew – Terry Morgan has wondered aloud if the measures lack rigour! 'I was a little concerned that some people might get complacent on getting their scores. They might end up thinking

they are living the values, when in fact this may not be the case,'
he says.

Benefits

If it is accepted that a change management process does indeed
change values and behaviours, there still remains one big measurement issue: whether these changes add up to competitive success.
As the change process proceeds inside the company, the external
world is very likely to be undergoing changes simultaneously.
Competitors won't be standing still and will also be working on
customer relations, innovation, team building etc. If a programme
does no better than stay even with the competition, then its economic yield could be zero.

This is where the rubber hits the road. People engaged in culture change need to feel that they are having an impact on objective measures of performance. If they don't, they lose faith pretty
quickly. There were two types of measurement used at BAe that
satisfied the link between culture change and the bottom line: the
values scorecard and the run-up in the stock price.

The values scorecard – an adaptation of the balanced business
scorecard concept – offers a more real-time picture of performance gains than is possible with traditional accounting measures,
based as they are on historical costs. Financial performance alone
is rather like using a rear-view mirror to steer a car, since financial
results are consequences or outcomes, not the drivers of business
activity. The balanced business scorecard identifies those relatively
few critical performance measures that drive a business's performance. BAe adapted the balanced scorecard framework for use with
the five values, all clearly important determinants of economic
outcomes, and created the appropriate metrics.

At first there was some opposition to this idea from some managers, on the grounds that value metrics would inevitably be 'soft'
and possibly unreliable. But in the end the critics were won over.
One thing that gives the values scorecard widespread respect is
that business unit results are regularly reviewed by the company's

executive and operations committees. To understand how the scorecard works, look at the illustration below, where we've listed some typical scorecard measures for each of the five values. The result is a tool that is simple enough for executives in the cockpit to use for flying the business, but comprehensive enough to allow an overview of each of the critical domains of Benchmark.

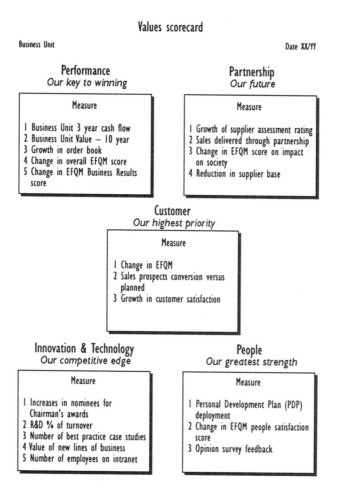

Values scorecard

Business Unit   Date XX/YY

Performance
Our key to winning

Measure

1 Business Unit 3 year cash flow
2 Business Unit Value — 10 year
3 Growth in order book
4 Change in overall EFQM score
5 Change in EFQM Business Results
  score

Partnership
Our future

Measure

1 Growth of supplier assessment rating
2 Sales delivered through partnership
3 Change in EFQM score on impact
  on society
4 Reduction in supplier base

Customer
Our highest priority

Measure

1 Change in EFQM
2 Sales prospects conversion versus
  planned
3 Growth in customer satisfaction

Innovation & Technology
Our competitive edge

Measure

1 Increases in nominees for
  Chairman's awards
2 R&D % of turnover
3 Number of best practice case studies
4 Value of new lines of business
5 Number of employees on intranet

People
Our greatest strength

Measure

1 Personal Development Plan (PDP)
  deployment
2 Change in EFQM people satisfaction
  score
3 Opinion survey feedback

The second approach that BAe used to measure benefits revolves around changed shareholder perceptions. During the four years of Benchmark, the company's market capitalisation soared from £1.3 billion to £8.7 billion in the weeks before the merger with GEC Marconi. It is impossible to estimate how much of this gain is due to Benchmark. In the perceptions of shareholders, the answer is zero, since they have never heard of it. They see the other value-creating events that have been occurring simultaneously: acquisitions, asset disposals, new joint ventures, order book fattening – the list is endless.

Even so, a management team that has laboured as hard and as long as BAe's at a very costly change management effort will nonetheless find some measure of validation in the share price. There is no consensus within BAe as to how much of the gain in overall efficiency is attributable to Benchmark. There are managers who say it is over half; others who think it is considerably less. Yet the even most laconic assessment of share value gains will come out with a number that is many, many times the programme costs.

You will recall that Dick Evans in the last chapter said that a 'bean counting', cost–benefit approach to a culture change programme is misguided. Similarly, it is short sighted to think that the sharp-eyed analysts in the City can begin to grasp everything that goes on inside a large, diffuse and complex organisation like BAe. Clever as they are, analysts cannot put a valuation on, for example, an improved leadership style, or different methods of organisation, though these are undeniably long-run determinants of success. What is the economic value of a sales manager who has spent all day in meetings, yet is so keen about customer service that he returns all his calls the same day instead of letting them slide till tomorrow or the next day? The answer is somewhere between a penny and a million pounds. Cumulatively, many such small acts do create an outcome that, when they are transmuted into cash flow, the stock markets acknowledge.

There will probably always be some sceptics about any positive correlation between culture change and share price. However, a recent study suggests that they are wrong. Professor Vinod Singhal of the Georgia Institute of Technology and Dr Kevin Hendricks of the College of William and Mary found that the 600 US companies that had effectively implemented TQM (total quality management) and won awards for their efforts outperformed a control group of non-award winners over a five-year period. TQM's emphasis on customer satisfaction, employee involvement and continuous improvement is sufficiently like a culture change programme for the study to be relevant here. These scholars found that the stock price of the TQM practitioners rose 119 per cent versus 75 per cent for the control group. Equally dramatic gains were recorded by the TQM companies in operating income, sales and total assets. 'The results of this study,' they say, 'indicate that effective adoption of performance excellence principles that are embedded in various quality award criteria do make good economic sense.'

That has certainly been the BAe experience. What is more, other research suggests that culture change is gaining in popularity in corporate management, notwithstanding its rather mixed accomplishments to date. A 1998 study by PricewaterhouseCoopers of the views of 400 chief executives of multinationals around the world found that an astonishingly large number of them are deeply involved in issues of behaviour. The survey found that much of the chief executive agenda went to such classic activities as setting vision and strategy and exploring mergers and acquisitions. But very nearly half the sample of chief executives lavished a great deal of their personal attention on reshaping corporate culture and employee behaviour; more attention than they did to another chief executive role, that of monitoring the company's financial information.

Culture change is getting on top management agendas for reasons similar to the situation of Dick Evans and BAe: often there is no other remedy for lagging corporate performance, neither a magic merger, nor reengineering or downsizing, nor reorganisation, nor the recruitment of a heroic leader from the outside.

Dear Dick

I have mixed views on the peer assessment proposal. On the positive side I think the concept is sound and it will reinforce the adoption of the values and the behavioural changes necessary to deliver the right results. I have to say, however, that the way we plan to implement left me feeling a bit uncomfortable. It came across as rather threatening and mysterious and in that sense incompatible with the aims of the people value. Why can we not simply incorporate the behavioural recognition issues into the 360 degree appraisal. In my view that population is much more informed than the proposed horizontal slice at peer group level.

***

Dear Dick

Whilst there may be some statistical validity in the averaging of inputs to peer assessment, I am of the view that to institutionalise 'secret' appraisals can only undermine the open, straightforward and truthful behaviours we wish to see demonstrated as part of the People Value.

***

Dear Dick

I was profoundly concerned about the ideas put forward for anonymous electronic scoring. I am a committed supporter of peer reporting. But I am convinced this has to be applied with openness, honesty, and the acceptance of personal responsibility for the comments made about peers. At worst it could degenerate into the sort of anonymous denunciation previously so prevalent in the former Soviet Bloc countries.

10
THE PAY-OFF

How far have we travelled to the promised land of Benchmark? How have we changed in the five years that we have been journeying? We ask ourselves such questions all the time, but the answers are elusive. Corporate culture change is oceanic, to be found in the spirit of the place, the quickness and eagerness of thought and of communication throughout the company. I can't prove that our people make swifter, smarter decisions, that their teamwork is better, that innovation and creativity at BAe are rising, but I sense it in the climate. And you'll have to take it on faith that I'm not delusional.

Let's imagine talking about Benchmark to one of the assembly teams in an aircraft hangar. I think the lads would say that they have heard the music of Benchmark. It sounds great in theory, but much of it remains a long way from their field of activity. Nevertheless, they will have observed changes that it has induced in their immediate environment and in the company's overall drive and vision and greater competence. For many manufacturing workers one visible facet of Benchmark is their team's Value Plan – which you will remember dovetails the separate plans of the team and the business unit and also fits in with the corporate plan. We are still rolling out the Value Plan, so it has not yet embraced everyone, but we've made giant strides.

'The Value Plan is one of the most powerful manifestations of

Benchmark,' says Mike Wills. 'If you go around the various businesses you will find a far greater number of people who have had an involvement with it. They understand the key objectives of their particular unit, and understand their personal role and how that contributes towards overall objectives. Three years ago you'd have found about ten people in each business unit with a knowledge of the value plan. Now it's hundreds and hundreds. And that is giving us all a commonality of purpose that never existed before.'

Moreover, many workers would acknowledge – continuing our imaginary factory tour – that BAe really seems to care about their personal and career development and individual fulfilment, thanks to Personal Development Plans (PDPs) and to the much improved job training and new learning opportunities that have sprung up across the company. Though not all will have signed up for the leased cars or the health scheme, everyone eligible has joined the share-ownership scheme. But I would hope that they would bear witness not only to formal processes that would have been unimaginable five years previously, but to an atmosphere of openness and good faith and to improved communication, within the teams and between team and team. The old BAe was beset by disconnections between people, between processes, between organisations, and the frustrations and angers that this unleashed. Benchmark has welded many of those disconnections and loose ends.

At the strategic level, Benchmark has unquestionably yielded tremendous competitive advantage, with further gains likely in the future. Five years ago when BAe was on the edge of extinction, our chief European competitors concluded that since their major competitor had receded, if not shrunk altogether, they could relax and look forward to enjoying a marketplace in which the damned Brits would not be around to be as arrogant as they used to be. For some time they failed to realise that we were struggling like hell to put the company to rights, and in the process substantially changing the whole way we did business. By the time they did wake up, we were well on our way to being the benchmark in our industry.

The German defence companies are beginning some of the things in culture change that we've been doing for a while. Our chief US competitors are formidable because of their size and the deep pockets of their principal customer, the Department of Defense, but they are (contrary to myth) far from being cracker-jack at productivity. I do worry that when they start going down the road we have travelled, as they inevitably must, we will see their competitiveness much improved. When they do awake, it will be with grim vigour and determination. They are sure to attack their considerable organisational fat. Lighter of foot and leaner, they will start sprinting, whereupon BAe will have to gallop hard to ensure that the turnover size gap between us does not widen.

Almost daily, I bump into instances of behaviour that would have been unimaginable in the old BAe. Here is one I found recently. Tom Nicholson and his team at Military Aircraft Division had become pretty zealous about best practice sharing. To his dismay, he found many blockers to a behaviour that everyone recognises as really important to Benchmark. His discovery is not exceptional; many innovative ideas and practices at BAe, acknowledged and celebrated, have not yet been widely adopted. 'We looked at two years of experience with the Chairman's Award for Innovation, company-wide and in our division, and found that absolutely tremendous ideas came from our people. But when we tracked their subsequent history, to see if the innovator's phone was ringing off the hook, we found that ideas were being neglected. I've come up with a modest proposal to remedy this: to take some recipients of the Chairman's Award and give them a sabbatical, to search out other areas of the business where their idea has applicability. And we will help them implement. We think that is quite a radical suggestion, giving people 12 months to go wander around the business in a structured way.'

Eureka moments

I have had several Eureka moments, where, like Archimedes in his bathtub, I suddenly said: 'Aha. This is Benchmark at work.' I'd like to share some of these instances when culture change unequivocally made a difference:

⬆ The very first Eureka was in 1996 when our losing turboprop JetStream division had to be shut down due to losses and poor market prospects. Some 600 people were faced with redundancy. Without any prompting, managers from many other business units called their counterparts at Prestwick, Scotland, where the Jetstream was made, and said: 'We understand your problem. What can we do to help? We have a number of vacancies coming up that perhaps could be filled by JetStream personnel.' Now that may strike you as simple common sense, unremarkable rational management behaviour. But the fact is that in the old BAe, the thought simply would not have occurred to anyone. Of the 600 initial possible redundancies at JetStream, the actual number came to around 200. More recently, in 1998 at Chatterton, there has been a similar need to shrink the workforce, and people from all over the company are offering to help and absorb Chatterton people. Previously, these human resources would have disappeared out of the company and we would have wasted them.

⬆ A second Eureka was winning the £3 billion Nimrod 2000 maritime patrol aircraft contract in 1996, against formidable US competition. For the first time we put together a pan-BAe bid team from several parts of the organisation. The bid was sponsored by Military Aircraft, but Prestwick, site of aerostructures and subsystem work, was deeply involved. So too were the people at our Filton site, whose role was to design and build a new wing for this aircraft. The finance people at our Farnborough headquarters also did sterling work: they came up with some very innovative ideas on financing to make the programme affordable to the Ministry of Defence, which happened to have a cash shortage scheduled for the main years when this programme would be in production. In the past Military Aircraft would have gone solo on this, and undoubtedly lost the deal. Nimrod is expected to create and sustain at least 10,000 UK jobs in the next 12 years. Parenthetically, it represents the wave of the future in terms of sophisticated technology. More than half the costs of one of the most sophisticated airborne systems in the world are in avionic packages and software.

🔺 In the spring of 1996, the managers in the 130 Group, spurred on by Kevin Smith, made a dramatic commitment to me. Over the next three years they would in aggregate deliver an additional £1 billion of value to the company on top of the gains expected from the established Value Plan. That was one hell of a starting point, a great moment of validation for Benchmark, because it demonstrated what I'd sensed when we set out on this journey: there were economic opportunities buried in the business that could be mined. The sources of this additional £1 billion (presented to me in the form of a giant-sized cheque) were winning more business, plus improvements in cycle time and inventories, plus better supplier relationships and strategic alliances and improved customer relations. In fact we exceeded the target. At year-end 1998 the number was around £1.5 billion.

🔺 My fourth Eureka example concerns organisational flexibility. When Benchmark was launched, the divisional cultures were so fierce and so protective that top management could not have merged any of them without provoking a near riot. However in 1997, for a variety of operational and financial reasons, we melded the Military Aircraft Division (MAD) with our Aerostructures Division, to form MA&A. The merger was trouble free, with almost no impact on the perceptions of customers and minimal effect on the bulk of the workforce. This happened because the management of each unit all had the one-company focus and all recognised the benefits that would ensue.

🔺 My last Eureka is something on the drawing board as I write, due to become effective in 1999, when about 5 per cent of the bonuses given to executive directors, and a slightly smaller percentage for other senior managers, will be directly tied to the statistical results of employee opinion polls. There is no better way to encourage behaviours that are conducive to communication, leadership, mentoring – the qualities that are measured by the opinion poll – than to put a carrot in front of an executive's nose. Up to now we've used every means of persuasion that imagination could devise to get the 130 Group to buy into

Benchmark. Now we will penalise and reward according to the observations of their subordinates. I suspect that there is not a big company in the country prepared to go this far down the path of linking employees' perceptions of leaders' behaviour to their economic merit.

My Eureka examples have one drawback. They fail to do justice to the vast array of Benchmark's primary and second-order effects that have become embedded in our conduct. These for the most part go unsung. It is from these tiny grains of sand that the bricks get built that construct the house. Up and down the company there is a quiet groundswell of changed conduct that is moving us towards unparalleled competitive strength.

The long journey

I don't want to leave the impression that Benchmark is an unqualified success. It isn't yet, because in some key areas it hasn't delivered the goods – in the customer value, for instance. At the UK Ministry of Defence there has been no sudden epiphany that we are a benchmark organisation. So far, we have merely convinced them that we now recognise our problems. Whereas hitherto we were incredibly arrogant towards them as a customer, we have shown determination to change, and here and there they see a glimmer of what might be. But they say, and rightly so, 'Now we need to see you deliver the results of your culture change.' This won't happen overnight. In this business it takes a long time for the results to actually come through. Today there is, genuinely, much more openness on both sides, therefore the relationship is healthier and more stable. That might not seem like much, but I see it as a giant stride, because it had been an exceedingly hostile relationship. And there are many other areas of performance where our aspirations in the values are not sufficiently realised in the real world.

Benchmark's achievement should be viewed in the context of the dark trough in which we began. It would be wrong to leave the impression that we have crossed the tape and are now at or beyond benchmark in most areas of performance like a General Electric, or a Hewlett-Packard, or an Intel or a Coca-Cola. But it is correct to say that within the defence and aerospace business we have demonstrated a prowess in culture change that is the envy of our rivals. When we set out to be a benchmark company, we left the end point of the transition deliberately vague. We didn't say that our target would be to win one of the coveted awards, like those from the EFQM or the British Quality Council. We wanted to be a company like the one we have become, where in everything we do there is this insistent question in the air: 'Are we benchmark on this?' And if we conclude that we're not benchmark but a laggard, then we promptly get cracking on the remedy. 'Being the best' has moved from being a high-stretch slogan to become the instinct of the organisation. 'The nice thing about Benchmark is that it is timeless,' notes Terry Morgan. 'We never will be benchmark. Because if we think we are the best we then look for someone better, just to keep up the challenge of continuous improvement.'

While Benchmark is a lot sturdier than it was, like any culture change programme it is delicate and in need of perpetual affirmation and a persistent going forward so that the forces of regression, which are never absent, don't take hold. A PricewaterhouseCoopers' study of 500 organisations that had gone through significant change found that the biggest barriers to change, as participants see it, emerge towards the end of the projects. At the launch stage, everyone is full of optimism and likely to feel the obstacles few and easily vanquished. One or two years later the mood is bleak: the easy quick wins (the celebrations of success) are far in the past, and participants see themselves surrounded by the debris of initiatives, they see one-time champions of change spluttering and poking along, the scale of the undertaking is daunting and suddenly it is no fun any more. To forestall any of these factors, I have not slacked off in my commitment, or ceased to make a public display of it.

As Robert L. Stevenson said, 'It is better to travel than to arrive.' What is at the end of the journey? The last milestone? It glimmers far in the distance. We will call Benchmark a total success only when all the things that we have talked about, all the values, all the behaviours have become an unconscious and spontaneous part of everyone's day-to-day behaviour.

My part of the tale is ended. It will be for my successor as Chief Executive, John Weston, appointed in the summer of 1998, to carry the Benchmark torch. While I play an active supporting role, he will continue the journey. From the beginning he has played a very influential role in shaping the characteristics of Benchmark, and he too has gone through some very positive behavioural changes. I'm sure he will do a great job fulfilling the promise of Benchmark. (He explains some of his new agenda in the Epilogue.)

We have made no secret of Benchmark. Yet up to now we have been so intent on developing culture change that (suppliers and customers excepted) the programme's existence is not well known. Consequently, many people outside BAe are unaware of the transformation that has been wrought. I was dismayed to see Matthew Lynn of the *Sunday Times* write in late 1998: 'BAe is one of the world's top armaments manufacturers, operating in an industry where people are not exactly required to get in touch with the caring side of their natures. It is a fiercely political, competitive world and BAe has always been a fiercely competitive, political company.' I don't mind our competitors thinking us fierce. As to the 'caring side of our natures', I'd like Mr Lynn to sit down with BAe executives. He'd find we no longer eat nails for breakfast and that we do show empathy and consideration to colleagues, not just to dogs and old ladies. For many of us who've been on this journey, some of our best experiences have been the enjoyment of getting to know and like people in other business units who are now friends and colleagues, not strangers any more.

It has been a long journey – a far longer experience than the calendar would suggest. No account of it would be complete without acknowledging the human stuff that went into it. This book has of necessity talked goals, programmes, outcomes. But none of these would have been possible without the willingness of many thousands of men and women across BAe to learn, reflect and to adapt to change. When we set out, I for one had no idea how demanding that adaptation would be, how deeply everyone in

Benchmark would be called on to question their personal values and behaviours. So I heartily salute and thank all those who've contributed to this transformation and encourage them to keep applying and enriching the Benchmark values.

EPILOGUE: THE FUTURE OF BENCHMARK

John Weston, Chief Executive

Having said just about everything that can be said about Benchmark, Dick Evans and Colin Price have generously left me the last word. The two authors have exhaustively covered the project from when it was but a gleam in Dick's eye to its present highly evolved state. It falls to me to predict the mutations that may occur in the future. There is one sense, however, in which Benchmark has arrived at one of its main destinations. After five intense years, Benchmark is becoming the essence of the way we run the company day to day. It is not, as some culture change efforts appear to be, an activity that is separate from the core. Benchmark is embedded in our notions of identity and purpose, it is not a bunch of 'soft' initiatives overlaid on the business. No operational activity exists that is not touched by the framework of the five values. Ask any member of our top management what it was like eight years ago, and what it is like today, and the response you would get is that there has been a pronounced step change in the ways we deal with each other internally – including relations between management and unions.

This said, I also think that Benchmark needs a shot in the arm, not the first in its brief history. Deliberately, our culture change has no blueprint. It contains a potential for improvisation, so we

can alter course from time to time. My agenda for the Benchmark
future includes:

↑ Improving profit margins with significant cost reductions, better asset utilisation and project management. Only then will we
extract the full profit potential from our record high £28 billion
order book.

↑ Increasing intra-business unit transfers of executives, the opti-
mal way to achieve more best practice sharing. Despite a lot of
urging and arm twisting by the corporate centre, in the last year
fewer than one-fifth of all new jobs have been filled in this way.
I improved this score at the senior management level on
becoming chief executive: of 22 senior moves I made, more
than half were cross-business. But this has to be emulated at
middle and lower-middle levels. The opportunities for the sharing of knowledge across the company are incredible, as is the
latent capacity to innovate far more aggressively than in the
past. Yet I must confess to a certain frustration. We have created
powerful values, actions and deliverers that assist with innovation, but the spread of best practice is still too slow.

↑ Better customer account management, with really coherent
contact between BAe people and our customers' organisations.
I'd like to see clear, measurable processes across the company
for setting targets for customer satisfaction.

↑ Our dreams of what we can get out of the technology and innovation value can exceed the reality by a big margin. There are
still instances of a parochial, 'not-invented-here' attitude.
There is a vast amount of knowledge close to shop and office
floors that should be transmitted and shared with others. I look
for the intranet to be a useful facility to further these aims.

↑ Drive harder at our established Value Based Management
methodology and embed it more deeply into decision making at
all levels. I suspect that there is much suboptimisation of profit
that needs to be rooted out of the business.

↑ A Coca-Cola executive at one of our seminars said, 'Change is
a thrill.' BAe is not there yet. Change unsettles us more than it

thrills us, an irony given the fact that we live in a particularly volatile industry. I'd like to see BAe people more secure as individuals and confident of their worth, even though the wallpaper and the furniture may be changing around us.

We've set ourselves up as the benchmark management team. Though this book is our first attempt to share what we've learned with whoever might be interested, word of Benchmark has spread in the business community as our results and share price have improved. Others seem to think that we are doing something right, and would like to know what. Throughout much of 1998 our share performance ranked number two or three among the FT-SE 100. To stay at that level, we have to consistently achieve returns in excess of 30 per cent – a formidable benchmark by any standard.

This achievement rests on the myriad accomplishments of BAe people, whose potential has been released and directed by Benchmark. In literally millions of instances over the years people have been able to act smarter and faster. Only a very few of these success stories filter up to the top. I would like to recount some of the stories I have been lucky enough to stumble across on visits to company installations.

⬆ At our Brough site, I toured a machine shop, escorted by a young operator with a ponytail and a gold earring. This man had been part of a multidisciplinary team of engineers, shop supervisors, operators and production planners that had installed a new profile milling machine. Setting up this operation had previously been a job for a qualified engineer, but the job was restructured and given to the operator. My escort showed me how the jobs got loaded on to the computer and demonstrated how last-minute changes could be made if needed – tremendously excited at the fact that his job had been enriched. As I left, a shop supervisor confidentially told me: 'This man has been through an amazing change. A year ago he had the worst attendance record on the floor. You wouldn't know it was the same chap.'

⬆ At Samlesbury, home of our state-of-the-art facility for Airbus wings, I met a team leader whose job it was to assemble a part for the A320's wings. Some time earlier his team had been rebuked for poor workmanship on this item. Stung by the criticism, he studied the problem and, after a lot of measurement and testing in his own time, found that the subcontractor was in fact supplying a part whose specs were wrong, to a degree imperceptible to the naked eye. At the next delivery, he asked the subcontractor to produce an engineer for a discussion about the specs. He then ran tests that convinced the engineer that there was a problem, and it was corrected immediately. There is no doubt in my mind that 10 years earlier this situation would have sparked a management–union dispute and been a case for a 'registered grievance', with the operators claiming that the rebuke on quality was unfair and blaming stupid management for procuring defective parts. It would have occurred to no one then that the problem could be owned by the team leader, diagnosed and remedied by him, and the sucessful outcome reported to management.

⬆ A floor sweeper in the final assembly area of our Avro regional jet facility at Woodford, Cheshire, noticed that many tools were not being well looked after by the operators. On his own initiative he found an unused office nearby and painted it in his own time with paint he paid for himself. He then found and moved in some surplus cabinets that were good for tool storage. He had created a tool repository. He made requisite tool registers and encouraged workers to use his facility, which they happily did.

⬆ The team working on the final assembly of our prototype of the first British Eurofighter 2000 had run over its budget for permissible overtime several months before the deadline. In the final weeks they clocked out at the regular time, then turned around and went back in to work without pay. Thereby they achieved two goals: they met the flight deadline, and they did not to exceed the overtime budget that, as a team, they'd been given to manage. Now that's what I call culture change!

Imagine similar stories occurring thousands of times a week, and you'll get an idea of the cumulative economic gain released in people by Benchmark, to say nothing of its effect on the improvement in process, communication, organisation and so forth. I'm convinced that we've just scratched the surface of the opportunities that Benchmark's reach and scale and excellence of design provide as it bites deeper into the fabric of our organisation.

While we've been labouring away at Benchmark, the company's external environment has been rocked by changes that are fundamentally redefining the industry. When we began Benchmark, we understood that a major reorganisation of global defence and aerospace production loomed over us all. This scenario was at the heart of our motives for embracing culture change, as I made clear in my 1995 report 'The Case for Change', which got a lot of our managers to recognise the logic of Benchmark. In recent years BAe has responded to the altered terrain with more joint ventures with rival manufacturers, several strategic acquisitions and some divestitures. Benchmark was not introduced into joint ventures conducted by independent stand-alone corporate entities, although we urged joint venture management to consider the merits of a programme of a similar stripe. (Incidentally, Airbus participated fully because a consortium, not a joint venture, makes its planes.)

Vertical Take-Off appears at a defining moment for the global aerospace industry. Over the next few years we will see the issue of a single corporate entity for Airbus resolved, plus new linkages by joint venture and merger between many, if not all, the European producers and the US players as well. Our views on these issues are well known, and in any event are outside the province of this book. But we are also very sensitive to the future of Benchmark as these possible restructuring scenarios unfold. Inside the company we have been asked the question, 'Will something as intangible as a culture change programme survive a merger? Won't Benchmark be diluted?'

No, because the language of profit is universal. When you have a culture change project that isn't just slogans and T-shirts and posters and flimflam, you have a very powerful asset; as powerful, I'll wager, as BAe's acknowledged skills in prime contracting and system integration capabilities. This 'technology' of culture change is hard to make work, but it is available to everyone and is in fact spreading through the corporate community. It would not be rational for a merger or joint venture partner to reject the knowledge that we have worked so hard to win. And should it turn out that they have better ideas on culture change, great – we'll adopt these too.

In summary, there are many problems for us entailed in the future restructuring and consolidation of the global defence industry, but Benchmark is not one of them. It is an ace among the cards we have to play. And this is the time to play it. We have a really fine cultural framework in place; now the company has to deliver world-class, sustainable performance. Only then will Benchmark fully live up to its name.

INDEX

130 Group 32, 34, 36, 39, 62, 66, 80, 86, 90, 104, 107, 129, 145, 149, 155, 157, 158–9, 163–5, 173–4, 176, 185, 187, 199
360° feedback 156, 160–61, 162
3M 73, 90

actions, Benchmark 106–31, 139
Aerostructures 68, 118, 124–5, 199
Airbus Industrie x, 14, 114, 115, 124, 208, 209
Al Yamamah contract vii, 7, 29, 45, 96
Allied Signal 55, 88, 92
Arlington Securities 6
Avro 68, 101, 125, 208

BAeSema 22
balance, finding 137–9
Bauman, Bob 7, 18, 20, 66, 92
Behaviour Recognition Matrix 187–8
behaviours 93–4, 97, 134, 139, 164, 175, 187, 190, 202
beliefs 48–9, 51
Benchmark
    actions 106–31, 139
    benefits of 12, 190–2, 195–203
    effects of 184–90
    future of 206–7
    implementation of 86–105
    infrastructure 148, 171–5
    objections to 13–14
    paradoxes of 130–31, 135–7
Benchmark Employer 120–21, 129
Benchmark Success Board 183–4
benefits of Benchmark 12, 190–2, 195–203
BEST (Benchmark Executive Skills Training) 148, 157–66, 176
BMW 142–3
Boeing 8, 9, 22, 102
Bossidy, Larry 55, 88, 92
British Airways 58
Brother 73
Burke, Warner 18, 36, 60–61
business drivers 140–44
Business Excellence Review 111–12

'Case for Change, The' 17, 26, 209
Chairman's Award for Innovation 74, 114–16, 129, 146, 197
change management 44–61, 86
Coca-Cola 55, 201
communications 94–5, 148, 175–6

competitive context 101–101
corporate culture 35, 48–52,
    90–91
culture change vii–viii, ix–x, 10,
    12, 14–17, 23, 26–7, 133–47
culture change, barriers to 65
culture change, resisting 134
culture change, when not advis-
    able 52–60
customer satisfaction process
    model 125–8
Customer Value Team 62, 66–70,
    112, 126
customer value 38, 125–8, 185

Dana Corp 169
defence industry rationalisation ix,
    8, 22, 90
deliverers 141, 148–77
Drucker, Peter 47

Eddie Bauer 169
effects, of Benchmark 184–90
EFQM (European Foundation for
    Quality Management) 71–2,
    111–12, 113, 144, 162, 201
employee car scheme 120–21,
    129, 196
Eurofighter x, 29, 115, 171, 208
Excel 120–21

Ford Motor 169
future, of Benchmark 206–7

Gardner, David 168
GE 47, 58–9, 61, 169, 201
GEC x, 2, 22, 142–3, 172
General Motors 169
Geoghegan, Chris 11, 12, 29

Glaxo Wellcome 55, 145
government relations, improving
    123–4

Hamlin, Mark 149–56, 159, 162
Handy, Charles 136
Hanson Industries 53
Harper, Mike 48
Harrier 68, 70
Hawk 128
Hawksworth, Roger 107
Hawtin, Peter 27, 158, 172–3,
    176, 189
health care scheme 120–21, 196
Hewlett-Packard 45, 73, 170, 201
history, of BAe 5–6

IBM 169
implementation, of Benchmark
    86–105
infrastructure, of Benchmark 148,
    171–5
Innovation and Technology Value
    Team 72–4
innovation and technology value
    38, 114–17, 185, 206
Innovation Forum 116
Intel 45, 55, 98, 201
internal consulting group 172–3
Internal Trading Framework
    124–5
intranet 117
involvement process 117–18

JetStream 198
joint ventures 122

Kawasaki Heavy Industries 73
Kenney-Wallace, Geraldine 170

Kubler-Ross, Elizabeth 152–3

Lapthorne, Richard 11, 24, 35, 71, 156
leadership development 148, 149–57
leadership 57–60, 95, 97–8, 102–4, 139, 144–6
'letters to Dick' 32–4, 40–43, 82–5, 132, 178–81, 189, 194
Lloyds Bank 145
Lockheed Martin 8, 22

Marconi Electronics ix, x, 22, 75, 142, 191
Matra BAe Dynamics x
McCarthy, Tony 46, 152
McDonnell Douglas 8, 102
Meakin, Rob 7, 18–19, 172, 174
Microsoft 55
Miles, Gerry 162
Military Aircraft and Aerostructures 127, 199
Military Aircraft 149, 171, 174, 197–9
Ministry of Defence 66–8, 101, 128, 198, 200
Mogford, Steve 11, 20, 26, 157
Morgan, Terry 24, 60, 108, 120, 175, 189, 201
Motorola 169

NatWest Bank 103
Nicholson, Tom 10, 27, 28, 34, 64, 79, 127, 197
Nike 55
Nimrod 171

objections to Benchmark 13–14

opinion surveys 185–7

paradoxes, of Benchmark 130–31, 135–7
partnering 74–5
Partnership Value Team 74–6, 124
partnership value 38, 122–5, 185
Peer Recognition Process 164, 185, 187–90
people practices 99
People Value Team 76–80, 107, 119, 120
people value 38, 117–22, 159, 185
performance measures 98–9, 181–93
Performance Value Team 70–72, 109, 166
performance value 38, 109–13, 166
Personal Development Plans 119–20, 129, 196
Pilkington's 54
Pratt, Lew 170
Price Waterhouse (now PricewaterhouseCoopers) 65, 134, 159, 161, 162, 193, 201
procurement improvement 122–3
profit sharing 121–2
purpose 99–100, 137

RAF 67–8
Rank Xerox 73
restructuring, of BAe 2–4
Rice, Tony 25, 37, 155
RJR Nabisco 48
role modelling 102–4, 139, 144–6, 164
Rolls-Royce 9, 58
Rose, George 88

Rouse, Mike 118
Rover 2, 6, 19, 142–3, 172
Royal Dutch/Shell 54
Royal Ordnance 6, 113, 114, 149, 172
Ryan, Locksley 29, 129–30

Schein, Edgar 51
share ownership scheme 129, 196
share price 2–3, 9, 12, 80, 190, 192
Siemens Plessey 22
Simpson, Lord George 143
Smith, Kevin 174–5, 199
SmithKline Beecham 92
Sony 73
Sowerby Research Centre 116, 170
Strategic Leaders Programme 148, 176
strategy 89–91, 99–100
structure 100–101

Team Based Value Planning 110, 166–7
Team Leader Training 148, 166–8, 176
top managers, meetings of 24–5, 27–30
Tornado 7, 171
Truman, Trevor 27, 138

Turnbull, Sharon 165
Turner, Damien 13, 37, 174
Turner, Mike 14, 19

US Patent Office 169

Value Based Management 112–13, 144, 206
Value Plans 111, 119, 166–8, 195–6, 199
Value Planning 109–11, 129
value shifts 97–102
Value Teams 39, 62–81, 107, 134
values scorecard 190–91
values 35–9, 48–9, 51, 80, 86–104, 106–7, 108, 137, 139, 157, 159, 161–4, 168, 185, 187, 190, 202, 203
Virtual University 148, 168–71
vision 30–32, 80, 99–100, 137, 139, 157

Wanless, Derek 103
Warton 27, 171
Welch, Jack 47, 58–9, 61
Welch, Jim 16
Weston, John 17–18, 26, 128, 144, 165, 202, 205–10
Wills, Mike 11, 63–4, 80
Wilson, Ray 28
Wooding, Jerry 9, 66, 70, 100